Oxford Shakespeare Topics

Shakespeare's Dramatic Genres

OXFORD SHAKESPEARE TOPICS
Published and Forthcoming Titles Include:

Oxford Shakespeare Topics

GENERAL EDITORS: PETER HOLLAND AND STANLEY WELLS

Shakespeare's Dramatic Genres

LAWRENCE DANSON

OXFORD

UNIVERSITY PRESS

OXFORD
UNIVERSITY PRESS

Great Clarendon Street, Oxford OX2 6DP
Oxford University Press is a department of the University of Oxford.
It furthers the University's objective of excellence in research, scholarship,
and education by publishing worldwide in

Oxford New York

Athens Auckland Bangkok Bogotá Buenos Aires Calcutta
Cape Town Chennai Dar es Salaam Delhi Florence Hong Kong Istanbul
Karachi Kuala Lumpur Madrid Melbourne Mexico City Mumbai
Nairobi Paris São Paulo Singapore Taipei Tokyo Toronto Warsaw

and associated companies in Berlin Ibadan

Oxford is a registered trade mark of Oxford University Press
in the UK and certain other countries

Published in the United States
by Oxford University Press Inc., New York

British Library Cataloguing in Publication Data
Data available

Library of Congress Cataloging-in-Publication Data
Danson, Lawrence.
    Shakespeare's dramatic genres / Lawrence Danson.
        p. cm.—(Oxford Shakespeare topics)
    Includes bibliographical references.
    1. Shakespeare, William, 1564–1616—Technique. 2. Shakespeare, William,
1564–1616—Philosophy. 3. Literature—Philosophy. 4. Drama—Technique. 5. Literary
form. I. Title. II. Series.
    PR2995 .D36 2000   822.3′3—dc21   99-048533

    ISBN 0-19-871173-5
    ISBN 0-19-871172-7 (pbk.)

3 5 7 9 10 8 6 4 2

Typeset by Kolam Information Services Pvt Ltd., Pondicherry, India
Printed in Great Britain
on acid-free paper by
Biddles Ltd., Guildford and King's Lynn

Contents

Illustrations

The photographs are reproduced by permission of Princeton University Library.

| *Note on Texts*

I have used *The Oxford Shakespeare* edition of *The Complete Works*, General Editors Stanley Wells and Gray Taylor (Oxford: Clarendon Press, 1988). The Oxford edition prints both the quarto and Folio texts of *King Lear*: all my citations are to the Folio text, which I designate F along with the act-scene-line numbers. I have restored the traditional names of the comic characters in *Henry IV* (for instance, Falstaff).

For all other old texts, I have modernized the spelling and, where necessary, the punctuation, even when I cite them from modern editions.

The Genres in Theory

In James Thurber's story 'The Macbeth Murder Mystery', a tourist finds herself in an English Lake District hotel with nothing to read but a paperback copy of *The Tragedy of Macbeth*. She is a great fan of detective fiction; *Macbeth* had mistakenly been shelved with the mystery novels: '"You can imagine"', she tells the narrator, '"how mad I was when I found it was Shakespeare."' But she perseveres in her reading, and soon she works it out: Macbeth and Lady Macbeth weren't mixed up in Duncan's murder at all; the ones you most suspect, she explains, '"are the ones that are never guilty"'. No, Macduff did it, Macduff killed the king. That night the narrator, challenged by the lady's interpretation, rereads the mystery of *Macbeth*, and by the next morning he has found an even better interpretation: '"Macduff is as innocent of those murders . . . as Macbeth and the Macbeth woman."' On his ingenious theory, derived, like hers, from the protocols of detective fiction, '"Lady Macbeth's father killed the king . . . old Mr. Macbeth, whose ambition it was to make his daughter Queen."' Flush with his critical triumph, the narrator announces that he will now try to solve the greatest mystery of them all:

My companion's eyes brightened. 'Then', she said, 'You don't think Hamlet did it?' 'I am', I said, 'absolutely positive he didn't.' 'But who', she demanded, 'do you suspect?' I looked at her cryptically. 'Everybody', I said, and disappeared into a small grove of trees as silently as I had come.[1]

Silly, of course. We know that Shakespeare doesn't work that way. Tragedy he wrote, not murder mystery: Agatha Christie isn't his kind of thing. And so with all of Shakespeare's works, whether tragedy, comedy, or history: they fulfil the expectations appropriate to their kind, play by the rules of their own game, and demand that we interpret them accordingly. Thurber's tourist just doesn't get it. But what about another reader who thinks that a play in which a bright, independent woman is compelled by her dead father's will to marry a smooth-talking fortune-hunter, and in which that woman, blind to her own oppression, expresses racist views about an African suitor, and joins with the rest of her Christian community in persecuting an old Jewish gentleman, estranging his daughter, stealing his money, denying him the right to worship his God as he pleases—what about the reader who thinks *The Comical History of the Merchant of Venice*[2] is the saddest story ever written? Shall we say that comedies just don't work that way? Shall we say, Shakespeare just doesn't do that kind of thing? Or shall we rather say, as this book will say, that the relationships among readers, writers, and the kinds of literature really are mysteries worth puzzling over.

For a start we will have to define our terms as precisely as an inherently elusive subject allows. We can begin with a couple of simplifying exclusions. Shakespeare wrote lyric poems (the Sonnets), narrative poems (*Venus and Adonis*, *The Rape of Lucrece*), and drama. Our concern is the drama, so we can affirm that there are plays and there are *kinds* of plays. Sounds simple enough, but already there are problems. They are problems as old as Aristotle, who began his *Poetics* with a similar distinction, proposing to discuss poetry itself *and* its various kinds or species. Or, to use the word critics since the eighteenth century have tended to use, its genres, as in the word generic. We know who made the plays: Shakespeare wrote *King Lear*; but who made *tragedy*, the genre of which it is a member? I can read the play, watch it, or perform in it. I recognize that each reading or performance differs from every other reading or performance: *King Lear* exists in no simple monumental way—but compared to the genre, to the idea of a class of plays to which *King Lear* belongs, *King Lear* is as palpably real as the Eiffel Tower. There is, after all, no DNA which proves that such individuals as Sophocles' *Oedipus Rex*, Seneca's *Thyestes*, Marlowe's *Doctor Faustus*, Racine's *Phèdre*, and Miller's *Death of a Salesman* belong to the same species as *King Lear*. But it is a real question whether *King Lear* would even be conceivable if the genre, the idea of tragedy, despite its indeterminacy of physical locus, did not exist.

But exist how? Do the major dramatic genres, tragedy and comedy, somehow precede the individuals? We often speak as if that were the case, for instance when we ask whether this or that play is *really* a tragedy, whether it actually *succeeds* as a comedy. Our language in those instances presumes that the genre is more readily recognizable than the individual play which we may or may not decide to grant entrance into it. The trouble is that everyone's got their own idea of how to recognize it. To a learned critic in the Renaissance, a play which mixes clowns with kings in its cast of characters forfeits its right to be called a real tragedy. So much for *Hamlet* with its gravediggers, and for *King Lear* with its Fool. Some people think they can know a tragedy (to stick for a moment with that most prestigious genre) by its formal, its internal properties, like the shape of its plot and the social status of its characters. Others claim to know it by its effect on the reader or audience. So one student, pursuing the affective route, says that a tragedy isn't really a tragedy if it doesn't produce what Aristotle called a catharsis. Another student, slightly embarrassed, says he doesn't think he's ever had a catharsis. A third student tries to reassure him by taking a formalist route: she thinks the catharsis happens not to the audience but within the plot itself, as an aspect of the play's form. We've latched on to one of the keywords in the discourse of tragic theory only to discover that we aren't sure which door it opens. Do we know the genre by its formal properties (what it looks like) or its affective properties (what it achieves in its audience)?

The same questions apply to comedy. Most of Shakespeare's comedies end in marriage or the promise of marriage, and with the reconciliation of at least some members of the cast of characters who had previously been at odds. For Shakespeare, it seems, a comedy is a play whose plot aims to achieve marriage and social harmony. Ben Jonson, Shakespeare's great contemporary, had, both in his critical writing and in his own plays, a different idea of the comic plot: his *Epicoene*, for instance, ends happily with an annulment. But whether we take Shakespeare's plot or Jonson's for the generic norm, we have left out of account what many people would presume is the first requirement for comedy, that it makes us laugh. Yes, comedy is a laughing matter, despite moralizing critics like Jonson himself, who claimed that 'the moving of laughter is a fault of comedy, a kind of turpitude, that depraves some part of a man's nature'.[3] (Fortunately, Jonson the playwright did not always listen to Jonson the critic.) Still, audiences are fickle, productions variable, and the volume of laughter can be a misleading indicator of a play's generic status. Hamlet is a very witty tragic hero, and a production of his play may produce more laughs per minute than a production of a comedy like, say, *Measure for Measure.* As with the tragic catharsis, so with comic laughter: what many people would take to be the definitive word for the genre leaves us uncertainly between the formal and the affective ways of knowing, of defining, the genre.

So: tragedy and comedy exist, but we we aren't sure *how* they exist. Are comedy and tragedy formal categories, signifying different structures of plot and characterization; or are they different theatrical strategies for producing different effects on an audience? Or—yet another possibility—are they philosophical categories, signifying different visions of the world, different ways of being in it? To these questions about definition we must add another: genres exist, but do they always exist in the same way? Or could they be culturally specific categories which change with the changing times, always recognizable yet always shifting with shifting currents of literary and cultural history? The idea may seem illogical: what good is a category if its defining characteristics, by which we recognize it as a category, do not remain constant? Brain-teaser it may be, but such a situation helps explain the power and usefulness of genre in the production and reception of literature, including Shakespeare's plays. How do genres exist? Not as unchanging essences but as sets of loose similarities among artworks widely separated in their historical and cultural assumptions. They exist, then, in a kind of circularity between the general and the particular, as ideas about genres influence the creation of specific works and as those works in turn revise a culture's ideas about genres.

The eighteenth century in England is sometimes called the period of neo-classicism. It was a period deeply under the sway of a version of genre-theory supposedly derived from the classical critics, from Aristotle to Horace; to some informed readers it seemed as though the genres were based not only on contingent similarities but on immutable rules discovered by the ancients, always applicable, not dependent on historical circumstance or individual innovation. In Alexander Pope's brilliant version of the idea, the rules of genre are identical to the rules of nature itself:

Those rules of old discovered, not devised,
Are Nature still, but Nature methodized;
Nature, like liberty, is but restrained
By the same laws which first herself ordained.
('An Essay on Criticism', Part I, 88–91)

But the greatest English critic of that period was the independent-minded Dr Samuel Johnson. And Johnson, noting that the artistic imagination does not like limitations and arbitrary distinctions, wrote that 'There is scarcely any species of writing, of which we can tell what is its essence, and what are its constituents; every new genius produces some innovation, which, when invented and approved, subverts the rules which the practice of foregoing authors had established'.[4] According to Dr Johnson, there are 'species of writing' but they are species without fixed essences because each great writer puts his or her own spin on the genre; in the process they both subvert the received 'rules' of the genre and create new possibilities for it. In Johnson's view, then, genres exist precisely as the history of their own subversions and revisions. In order to know what has been subverted and revised, we must have an idea of the general class; to understand what interesting new thing the particular work of art is accomplishing, we must understand it precisely as a variation on the kind of thing it is. Genre, then, is a system in which each new member changes the system: a form always in the process of reforming itself. The genre of a work is an idea we maintain in order to recognize the work's affinity with or, just as importantly, its distance from other works, while simultaneously we recognize that the idea—of tragedy, of comedy, or any other genre—is never equal to the shifting reality of actual theatrical or literary practice.

We know an individual work—recognize its particularity and interpret its 'meaning'—partly by recognizing the extent to which it conforms to or diverges from previous generic practice. Take, for an extreme instance, the case of *Troilus and Cressida*. Critics have had a notoriously hard time knowing what to make of it. Shakespeare turns the cataclysm of the Trojan War into a deadly brawl between macho fools fighting for possession of a bimbo. Heroes are in very short supply, and women—Cressida as well as Helen—are made into whores by the very men who insist on fighting over them while claiming that whores aren't worth fighting over. It is a world where time itself is 'a great-sized monster | Of ingratitudes' (3. 3. 141–2) who gobbles up the past so quickly that good deeds are forgotten as soon as they are done; where merely going on, for good or ill, is the only alternative to being stomped into oblivion by the stampeding herd of history. It's not a pretty picture, this world of disease and decay, of betrayal and brute strength. Yet the prefatory note (not by Shakespeare) to its first edition describes *Troilus and Cressida* as a witty comedy fit to be compared with the funniest plays of the Roman playwrights Plautus and Terence. The prefatory note is the equivalent of advertising copy, and we don't have to believe every word of it. *Troilus and Cressida* does not end with marriage and reconciliation, and it certainly is no laugh-riot. It isn't in the same ball-park as Plautus and Terence. But does that mean it is playing tragedy's game instead?

That was the assumption made by the poet and critic John Dryden in the late seventeenth century. Overall, Dryden thought *Troilus and Cressida* was a good play, but because he expected it to conform to his idea of tragedy he could not approve of its ending: 'The chief persons, who give name to the tragedy, are left alive; Cressida is false and is not punished.'[5] By Dryden's standards, the definition of tragedy requires the death of its protagonists: if Romeo and Juliet, Hamlet, Lear, Macbeth, and all the rest die at the end of their tragedies, what (except Shakespeare's failure to do the right thing) can excuse the liveliness of Troilus and Cressida at the end of their tragedy? And by Dryden's standards, a tragedy ought to show the workings of Christian morality and divine providence. A play in which Cressida does not get what Dryden thinks she deserves cannot, by his definition, have an appropriately tragic ending. We notice that Dryden has brought to bear two of the most common standards for judging works of art: the play's ending is a failure on *formal* ground because the protagonists aren't dead, and it is a failure on *moral* grounds because a wicked character isn't punished. Even if Dryden reversed his initial assumption that the play is striving unsuccessfully to be a tragedy and assumed instead that the play is striving to be a comedy, still his two standards, moral and formal, would find the ending deficient: the heroic Hector is killed, and the chief persons are left unrewarded by marriage.

Must we conclude that *Troilus and Cressida* is either a failed comedy or a failed tragedy? Or is *Troilus and Cressida* rather a play which defines itself by its significant relationship to and distance from both genres? The manifest power of the play suggests the latter: that *Troilus and Cressida* is a stringent examination of the values which inform both comedy and tragedy. Its refusal to end in the expectable manner calls into question the very notion of how things end in drama. It invokes our desire for tragic finality, the *consummatum est* which, however terrifying, reassures us that something of great consequence has been achieved; and simultaneously it invokes our desire for comic renewal, the ending which is also a new beginning. In Samuel Johnson's words, the play 'subverts the rules which the practice of foregoing authors had established'. But in order to recognize the dramatic point of that subversion we have to see *Troilus and Cressida* in relation to the genres it simultaneously invokes and revises.

Which is not to say that some plays that at first look like mistakes won't always look like mistakes: 'bad play' is not a genre but it is a real category. But for us, as we begin to think about Shakespeare's genres, the point to be carried forward is that Shakespeare's plays are so many explorations and experiments in the endlessly revisionary process of genre-formation. The genres to which they belong are not prefabs but the diverse products of 'tradition: a sequence of influence and imitation and inherited codes connecting works in the genre'.[6] In the next chapter we will look at the theatrical scene in which Shakespeare located himself, and see how Shakespeare responded to the revisionary process as it was carried on by some of his predecessors and contemporaries. Later, and more extensively, we will look at the ways in which Shakespeare restlessly revisited and revised his own experiments with generic forms. Shakespeare's plays refer back and forth among themselves, endlessly invoking and endlessly complicating the genres they simultaneously inherit and make.

Creating the Categories

For now, we'll continue to think about Shakespeare and the problems of genre and classification. The modern student of Shakespeare cannot avoid them; often they are the unspoken reason why whole classrooms full of smart people fail to agree on the most basic interpretative issues. But you do not have to be an advanced student of the theory and history of genre in order to talk the talk. We use the terms of genre every day, and can, presumably, understand those terms when we hear them used by others. Here, for instance, is what a very loose idea of genre sounds like in Hollywood: 'Mr. Cameron described *Titanic* as "an epic romance set against an historical tragedy... My first goal is to create an overwhelming cathartic emotional experience for the audience.... It's a true love story."[7] It's a mish-mash of terms—epic, romance, history, tragedy, 'love story', and a *catharsis* thrown in for good measure. The genre words are vaguely used, overlapping and contradictory. With them the writer-director-producer assures us that *Titanic* isn't just the most expensive movie ever made: it's a classy movie, associated with as many culturally high-minded genres as possible.

Hollywood did not invent the mish-mash of genre-labelling. Elizabethans also needed the terms of differentiation even when they used them, as James Cameron uses them, to produce only a vague or potentially contradictory set of distinctions.

The problem confronts us, literally, on the first page. In 1623, seven years after Shakespeare's death, the actors John Heminges and Henry Condell edited the book that scholars now call the First Folio but that the title-page calls *Mr William Shakespeare's Comedies Histories and Tragedies* [Fig. 1]. The title signals the editors', and presumably Shakespeare's, allegiance to the idea that there are not just plays but kinds of plays, each kind with its conventions for composition and reception, and that the distinctions matter. But right there, in the editors' attempt to impose an order on Shakespeare's variety, we see how a system of genre can unsettle the very distinctions it is trying to stabilize: between the classically sanctioned pair Comedy and Tragedy comes a relative newcomer, History. (Aristotle recognized no such distinct category and, as we'll see, Shakespeare's contemporaries were also uncertain whether to think of 'history' as a sub-category of tragedy or as a term that subsumes both comedy and tragedy or as a distinct kind in its own right.) And if Heminges and Condell admit 'history', why not push for greater precision by recognizing even more kinds? Why not go all the way with Polonius, who tells Hamlet that the actors at Elsinore are the best in the world for 'tragedy, comedy, history, pastoral, pastoral-comical, historical-pastoral, tragical-historical, tragical-comical-historical-pastoral' (2. 2. 398–401)? A comprehensive system like his would undo itself, the attempt at precision reproducing the chaos of individuation it seeks to govern.

Mr. WILLIAM
SHAKESPEARES

COMEDIES,
HISTORIES, &
TRAGEDIES.

Publifhed according to the True Originall Copies.

LONDON
Printed by Ifaac Iaggard, and Ed. Blount. 1623.

1. The title-page of the First Folio (1623), the earliest collected edition of Shakespeare's plays. The compilers, Shakespeare's fellow actors John Heminges and Henry Condell, chose to assign each play to one of three genres, sometimes in a way which conflicts with its description in earlier, quarto editions and even with its individual title-page within the Folio itself.

Short of that disaster there is still the problem, even within a limited system like the one on the Folio title-page, of knowing where to place any given work, since to place it you must know what conventions it is invoking, but to know what conventions it is invoking you have to know what kind of thing it is. Like the modern Hollywood producer, Shakespeare's contemporaries commonly used the terms of genre in ways that demonstrate both their interest in generic distinctions and the difficulty they have in using them consistently. Eighteen of the Folio's thirty-six plays had previously been published in separate quarto editions. The title-page of the quarto version of *King Lear* calls the play a 'Chronicle History'; the Folio's title-page calls it *The Tragedy of King Lear*. Both the quarto and the Folio versions of *Richard III* call it a tragedy, but Heminges and Condell group it with the histories. *Troilus and Cressida*, which is called a comedy in the quarto's prefatory note, is called *The History of Troilus and Cressida* on its title-page, but in the Folio it becomes *The Tragedy of Troilus and Cressida*. The situation is the same with other playwrights. In 1567–8 a publisher registered his intention to bring out *A Tragedy of Apius and Virgine*; presumably it is the same play actually published in 1575 under the title *A New Tragicall Comedie of Apius and Virginia*. A foreign visitor to London in 1599 'reported that he "saw the tragedy of the first Emperor Julius [Caesar] with at least fifteen characters very well acted. At the end of the comedy", he continued, "they danced according to their custom"'.[8] This isn't just a foreigner's mistake: the word 'comedy', which designates a specific genre, was also sometimes used as the general word for *any* narrative. History is another such flexible word, capable of designating the particular and the entirely general. As Heminges and Condell use it, 'history' is a specific category, distinguished from either comedy or tragedy. But in *The Taming of the Shrew* the drunken tinker Christopher Sly is told that comedy 'is a kind of history', while George Whetstone, in his epistle to *Promos and Cassandra*—Shakespeare's principal source for *Measure for Measure*—writes, 'I have divided the whole history into two comedies'.[9] Indeed: there are comical histories (as the quarto's running headlines call *The Merchant of Venice*), tragical histories (as the quarto title-page calls *Hamlet*), and, yes, even history histories.

Such nominal instability does not necessarily prove the inability of either the theories or their practitioners to account for all the kinds of actual plays. It may suggest instead that Shakespeare's contemporaries had a healthy ability to live comfortably with the unruliness of a theatre where genre was not static but moving and mixing, always producing new possibilities. They did know the difference between comedy and tragedy and, like us, could use the terms as shorthand. So Robert Greene at the end of his prose romance *Pandosto* has some bad news (a suicide) to tell us along with the good (a marriage) or, as he puts it, has 'to close up the comedy with a tragical stratagem'.[10] The idea is clear enough—happy events are comic and sad events are tragic—but, in the very neatness of its parcelling out, also limiting. Shakespeare would deal more subtly with the combination of tragedy and comedy when he drew on *Pandosto* as the principal source for *The Winter's Tale*. In that play, we do not get a little of this and a little of that, first the sad and then the happy, but a vision of tragedy always implicit within the comic movement, of a tragicomedy which is more than the sum of its parts. Some classically minded critics despised the idea of tragicomedy: it was not a genre, they thought, but (in Sir Philip Sidney's contemptuous phrase) a 'mongrel'.[11] But in practice most Elizabethan playwrights and audiences knew that the genres inevitably do meet and recombine.

The Folio's tripartite division—comedy, history, and tragedy—has been basic to our thinking about Shakespeare for hundreds of years (Fig. 2). Imprecise and logically vexed though it is, it remains fundamental to our ways of reading, performing, and teaching Shakespeare: whole syllabi, whole vast shelves full of critical books, rest on that shaky foundation. But there is a little bit of Polonius in all genre critics, and we must observe, along with the tendency to preserve the Folio division, the critical tendency to multiply categories. To Heminges and Condell's three kinds, nineteenth-century critics added a fourth, 'romance': now virtually canonized, the word applies to the last-written of Shakespeare's plays. Of those, *Pericles* was not printed in the Folio, and the title-page of its quarto edition skirts the genre issue by calling it simply a 'play'. *The Tempest* and *The Winter's Tale* appear in the Folio as comedies, with *The Tempest* printed first in that group and *The Winter's Tale* concluding it. *Cymbeline* is printed as the last of the tragedies. And *Henry VIII*, a collaborative work which some critics include among the romances, is printed as the last of the histories, although its prologue describes 'the famous history' in terms

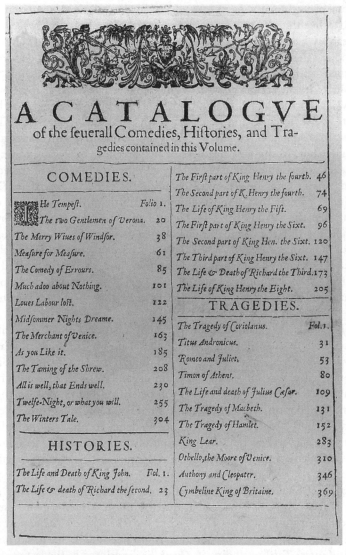

A CATALOGVE

of the feuerall Comedies, Hiftories, and Tra-
gedies contained in this Volume.

2. The 'catalogue', or table of contents, of the First Folio, with *The Tempest* listed first among the comedies, *Cymbeline* last among the tragedies. *Troilus and Cressida*, although it is printed in the Folio, failed to find its way into the table of contents. Several of the plays classified here as histories were elsewhere classified as tragedies.

traditionally used for tragedy. Modern critics have classified these late plays as a group, the romances, for several reasons. Although they are like the comedies (they end in reconciliations which include marriages and the repair of broken marriages, and with the promise of new beginnings through birth and dynastic succession), they are separated by several years—and several tragedies—from Shakespeare's earlier comedies. And they feel different from the earlier comedies. Their reclassification as a separate genre can be useful in bringing these facts to our attention, and in this book I will continue to use the name 'romance'. But I will treat the romances not in a chapter of their own but, when appropriate, along with the comedies or the tragedies. Separating them out too rigidly risks obscuring the ways in which the last plays are examples of Shakespeare's continual experimentation, his variation, revision, and subversion of his own and his contemporaries' idea of generic practice. The elements which compound one of his earliest plays, *The Comedy of Errors*—voyages over perilous seas to mysterious lands, the separation and eventual reunion of families, a sense of wonder approaching the realm of miracle—are the elements of *The Tempest* as well. True, much has changed between *The Comedy of Errors* and *The Tempest*; but both the change and the continuity are best observed when we allow our categories to remain broad enough to accommodate Shakespeare's innovations within them.

To comedy, history, tragedy, and now 'romance', critics in the first half of the twentieth century introduced yet another category, the so-called 'problem play'. The contents of the category change with each critic: *Troilus and Cressida*, *All's Well that Ends Well*, and *Measure for Measure* always make it in, while other leading contenders have included *The Taming of the Shrew*, *The Merchant of Venice*, *Antony and Cleopatra*, and (inevitably) *Hamlet*. Sometimes they are linked thematically, as plays which deal with difficult, even unseemly, social or philosophical issues; like the modern problem plays of Henrik Ibsen (whose work influenced the emergence of the category in critical discourse) they are plays which put dilemmas into action, unfolding and complicating them but refusing to resolve them. Sometimes they are linked formally, as plays which make problems for anyone attempting to fix them in one genre or another: they are comedies (for the most part) but only sort-of, not funny enough or happy enough or resolved

enough to be comedy-without-qualification. Again, there is value to
the category. It lets us see that some plays are troublesome precisely
because they aim to cause trouble; that not fitting easily into a tight
generic mould can be a virtue rather than a defect. If *Measure for
Measure* succeeds as a 'problem play', then we don't have to think
of it as an inexplicable failure to provide the pleasures of, say, *As You
Like It*.

But Heminges and Condell did not need a separate genre to see
that. And the 'problem play' category has now, I think, outlived its
usefulness. Ideas about Shakespeare's genres entail ideas about gender,
sexuality, and politics; about marriage within a patriarchal regime;
about monarchy and other forms of social organization; about all the
ingredients that would make a play's ending normatively happy or
unhappy. An historical understanding of sixteenth- and seventeenth-
century views of sex, marriage, and politics is essential to an historical
understanding of sixteenth- and seventeenth-century views of genre.
But the ideas Shakespeare received, about gender and genre, about
power and poetry, he literally put into play: his characters question the
presumably unquestionable, destabilize even what they affirm.
(Katherine at the end of *The Taming of the Shrew* gives a long sermon
on the desirability of wifely obedience: nothing could be more clear or
explicit, but we will never have done debating whether she, or Shakespeare, means it.) In that dramatic process, all Shakespeare's plays
become problem plays, even if some seem in certain eras to be more
insistently problematic than others. That leaves us with either a single
genre or with thirty-seven (or more) genres, each play its own problem, its own category-of-one. Or, more sensibly, it leaves us with the
Folio's discriminatory but not over-fussy division into comedy, history,
and tragedy.

The Folio's authority is so strong, in fact, that the strangeness of
some of its generic choices can pass unrecognized. By assigning each
play to a single kind the Folio obscures the fact that some plays might
go equally well in another, or that a single play might belong to more
than a single kind. Why, for instance, is *Macbeth*—a play, drawn from
historical sources, about a tyrant's rise to power, his downfall and
death—a tragedy, while *Richard III*—a play, drawn from historical
sources, about a tyrant's rise to power, his downfall and death—a
history? There is nothing inevitable about the distinction and, as we've

seen, Shakespeare's contemporaries were capable of cutting up the pie differently. One of those contemporaries, a scholarly parson named Francis Meres, assumed that all drama had to be divided into two, not three, parts. In 1598 Meres published a work of stupefying tediousness called *Palladis Tamia: Wit's Treasury*: over 300 pages of comparisons and analogies between anything and anything else, beginning with God ('As there is but one sun that enlighteneth the day... so there is but one God, that illuminateth the world') and ending with hell ('As God made heaven for good men, so he made hell for wicked men').[12] Meres's method of fantastic comparisons was the height of literary fashion; it is of interest to us for two reasons. First, this characteristically Elizabethan habit of mind, which discovers patterns, whether of likeness or difference, among all phenomena, is the same habit that makes genre-theory, with its ability to generate patterns of likeness and difference, so central to Renaissance thinking about literature. Second, Meres's book is of interest because one of the terms of his comparisons is the playwright William Shakespeare.

There were, says Meres, writers in Greece and Rome, and there are writers in England, and they are alike (to echo Shakespeare's Fluellen) as my fingers are to my fingers. For non-dramatic poetry, Meres compares 'mellifluous and honey-tongued Shakespeare' to 'sweet, witty Ovid'. And 'As Plautus and Seneca are accounted the best for comedy and tragedy among the Latins, so Shakespeare among the English is the most excellent in both kinds for the stage'. (Meres compares a whole host of English writers to the Greeks and Romans, but Shakespeare is the only English writer who gets marks equally for tragedy and comedy.) Meres then gives a list of Shakespeare's work 'in both kinds'—a list which scholars have found valuable for establishing a chronology of composition. For comedy, Meres asks us to 'witness his *[Two] Gentlemen of Verona*, his *[Comedy of] Errors*, his *Love's Labour's Lost*, his *Love's Labour's Won* [?], his *Midsummer Night's Dream*, and his *Merchant of Venice*'.[13] For tragedy, the list is more surprising: *Richard II, Richard III, Henry IV, King John, Titus Andronicus*, and *Romeo and Juliet*. To Meres, Shakespeare's tragedies were, apparently, indistinguishable from his histories. We need not decide whether Meres, who conflates tragedy and history, or Heminges and Condell, who distinguish between them, is correct. The point is that the divisions are provisional descriptions of practices which might be described in other terms as well; and that the mixing of modes is as important to Renaissance practice as is their separation.

From the earliest days of his writing career, then, Shakespeare was exploring the kinds of drama and, in the process of exploration, remaking them. The exploration discovers unexpected potential in received forms. In *Love's Labour's Lost* the comic resolution is relegated to a future the performance will never reach, a consummation ever to be devoutly wished. Shakespeare is not confused or uncertain about the theoretical requirements of genre, in this play or others we will look at; rather he is using those requirements as the stuff from which to wring surprise, playing across as well as within the lines of expectation, and showing the creative potential of a system of genre capable in his hands of generating, at any moment, new forms and new meanings out of old.

Contemporary Theory

In order to see those creative variations we need first to have a picture of the theory which neither Shakespeare nor any other first-rate contemporary playwright ever followed with slavish precision. Such a picture, literally, exists. In 1616, the year of Shakespeare's death and seven years before Heminges and Condell published the Folio, Shakespeare's greatest theatrical contemporary personally oversaw the publication of the book he grandly called *The Works of Benjamin Jonson*. The engraved title-page of Ben Jonson's folio is a pictorial essay on the dramatic kinds; it reads as both a history of the kinds through time and a statement of their presumably unchanging relations.

In pillared archways on opposite sides of an architectural façade stand the personified figures of Tragedy and Comedy [Fig. 3]. Though equal in size they are not equal in social status. Tragedy wears the costume appropriate to a lofty manner and matter: an embroidered gown, the high shoes (buskins) of the Greek tragic actor, and a crown; she carries a royal sceptre; behind her is an elaborately embroidered curtain; and on the pillar to her right hangs a mask with martial helmet. Across the way stands Comedy, in plain gown and socks; she is hatless and carries a rustic staff; behind her is an undecorated curtain, and to her left is a mask with a simple bonnet. Tragedy looks

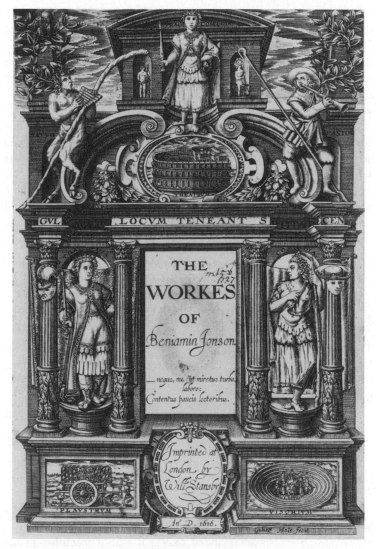

3. Ben Jonson oversaw the production of his collected *Works* (1616). The engraved title-page places Comedy and Tragedy in separate niches, and quotes Horace's injunction that each kind of writing should observe its own special decorum. The page reflects classical genre-theory as it was understood by Jonson's (and Shakespeare's) learned contemporaries.

regally out of the picture to a point somewhere over the viewer's right shoulder, while Comedy looks across the façade at Tragedy with (is it fanciful to imagine?) an invitingly come-hither glance and gesture. But the strong verticals of the columned façade suggest what is explicitly stated on the frieze above them: it is a line from Horace's *Art of Poetry*, 'Let each kind stay in its own appropriate place' (*Singula quaeque locum teneant sortita decenter*), the motto of literary decorum.[14]

On Jonson's title-page, the distinction betweenTragedy and Comedy is represented in historical terms by the scenes of their supposed origins. On the pedestal beneath Tragedy a horse-drawn cart moves across a rocky landscape. At the rear walks a tethered goat; a jug of wine hangs above the goat; and inside the cart—which looks like a portable prison—is a lone man: many of Jonson's readers would recognize him as the original thespian, and know that this is the historical moment described by Horace (in Jonson's own translation):

> *Thespis* is said to be the first found out
> The Tragedy, and carried it about,
> Till then unknown, in carts, wherein did ride
> Those that did sing, and act: their faces dyed
> With lees of wine.[15]

The word 'tragedy', they would know from the same source, derives from Greek *tragos*, 'the vile goat' which was, according to Horace, the tragedian's reward—or, possibly, the sacrifice to Dionysus, tragedy's tutelary god.

Comedy's origins are a lot less lonely and threatening: in a circular outdoor 'viewing place' (*visorium*) a chorus dances around a flaming altar. We are looking at the *komos*, the festive ritual of community, from which comedy supposedly takes not only its name but its nature. Like the figure of Comedy herself, comedy's originary scene is open and welcoming.

All this is clear enough; less clear is its relevance to actual Elizabethan dramatic practice. The apparently perverse refusal of English playwrights, Shakespeare included, to keep the kinds decently separate from one another was a commonplace of Elizabethan criticism. Rather than follow the exclusive decorums of style, subject, and character, they would, as Sir Philip Sidney complained, mingle 'kings and clowns, not because the matter so carrieth it, but thrust in clowns by head and shoulders, to play a part in majestical matters, with neither decency nor discretion'.[16] (Sidney was not entirely consistent about the decorum of the genres: writing of non-dramatic poetry, he notes that 'some [poets] have coupled together two or three kinds, as tragical and comical', and approves of the practice, 'for, if severed they be good, the conjunction cannot be hurtful.')[17] Such promiscuity is part of the joke in *A Midsummer Night's Dream*, where Peter Quince and his company of amateurs present 'A tedious brief scene of young Pyramus | And his love Thisbe: very tragical mirth'. Theseus knows that merry *and* tragical is 'hot ice and wondrous strange black snow' (5. 1. 56–9). What he does not know is that he himself inhabits a play which breaks the decorum of classical genre-theory: it has its appropriately clownish characters— and 'clown' in this context means both a funny person and a person of low social status, as if to be the one entails being the other; but the cast of characters ascends where comedy is not supposed to go, past the mighty Duke Theseus himself and right up to a king and queen. Shakespeare is breaking an ideal of decorum as surely as are his rude mechanicals, and his joke depends on our knowing it. And throughout the canon he challenges the decorum of social separation: Hamlet has his clownish gravedigger, Lear his Fool, and the monstrous Caliban can on occasion speak (to his sorrow) with an eloquence equal to that of the courtly Europeans who have washed up on his island.

Even on the Jonson title-page, once our eye ascends above the rigid verticals of the façade's lower two-thirds, we find a degree of complexity that can challenge strict hierarchy. For above Horace's injunction that each kind should keep its appropriate place, the picture's lines begin to bend inwards. Placed on Tragedy's side of the picture, as a sort of adjunct to her, is the rough and hairy goatish figure called Satyr, associated both in name and manner with satire, and on Comedy's side is the shepherd (*Pastor*) of pastoral poetry, with his pipe and crook. The Satyr's staff bends towards a foreshortened figure representing the god Dionysus (the god of wine and strong passions, traditionally associated with tragedy), the Shepherd's crook bends towards a figure of the god Apollo (associated with music, law, and comedy). At the top of all is a precariously perched figure labelled Tragicomedy: there it stands, the form Sir Philip Sidney called a 'mongrel', crowned like Tragedy but with the socks of Comedy, either uniting what art and nature were supposed to have separated or—it depends on the viewer's judgement—about to tumble off the page from a niche too small to accommodate it. In 1616 tragicomedy was the height of theatrical fashion: the writing-team of Beaumont and Fletcher were especially successful at it, but Shakespeare's own last plays, the ones we call romances, were also of that mixed kind. Jonson himself had written part of a pastoral tragicomedy. Jonson's theoretical scene risks self-contradiction by taking into account the facts of his historical moment, when aesthetic combination rather than separation was in critical vogue. Like Polonius's over-zealous effort, so even Ben Jonson's effort to produce a scene of theoretical clarity begins to reproduce the wildness of theatrical fact.

One complicating element is satire. Ben Jonson places satire on the tragic side of his genre-picture. But in the plays of Shakespeare and his contemporaries, satire is everywhere. It infiltrates both comedy and tragedy. Flamineo and Bosola in John Webster's tragedies *The White Devil* and *The Duchess of Malfi*, Malevole in Marston's *The Malcontent*, Vindice in *The Revenger's Tragedy* are satirists, railing against the corruption of the world yet trapped within the social system they condemn: like Hamlet, with whom they are close kin, they curse the spite that ever they were born to set the world right. Plays like Webster's and Marston's, and like *Hamlet* itself, are often placed by modern critics in the sub-category 'revenge tragedies'; they might just as reasonably be called tragical satires. But the sour spirit of the mocking satyr makes itself at home in the comic landscape as well. Jonson designated three of his own plays as 'comical satires'. Even in the nominally gentlest of Shakespeare's comedies, *As You Like It*, the character of Jaques is the character of the stage-satirist, demanding 'as large a charter as the wind, | To blow on whom I please . . . To speak my mind, and . . . through and through | Cleanse the foul body of th'infected world' (2. 7. 48–9, 59–60). Jaques's presence in Arden challenges comedy's claim to happy inclusiveness as surely as Hamlet's grave-digger challenges tragedy's claim that death is an ennobling consummation devoutly to be wished.

In its picture of the physical theatre itself, Jonson's title-page acknowledges the splendidly messy reality of generic innovation and instability. In the oval frame between Satyr and Pastor is a Roman theatre, semicircular, pillared, and built of stone, except that its open end is occupied by a wooden structure which resembles the stage-canopy and backstage area of an Elizabethan theatre. Neither Jonson nor his engraver is ignorant of the history of architectural styles. Jonson's theatre, in its combination of classical and modern forms, visually pronounces drama's creative treatment of the traditional and the new, its reshaping the precedents of classical genre-theory to the requirements of its age. Elsewhere, Jonson nicely sums up his attitude to the reborn art and ideas of Greece and Rome, an attitude he shared with the best Renaissance scholars and artists: 'I know of nothing [that] can conduce more to letters than to examine the writings of the ancients, and not to rest in their sole authority, or to take all in trust from them ... It is true, they opened the gates, and made the way, that went before us; but as guides, not commanders'.[18]

Origins of Genre-Theory

Who were the guides of Shakespeare and the other playwrights who looked with reverence at the classical past even as they exercised their own creative freedom? Where did their theoretical picture of the theatrical scene come from? In the rest of this chapter we'll glance at the chequered history of genre-theory. In the next chapter we'll look more closely at the actual stage practice of Shakespeare's predecessors and contemporaries. Theory and practice were never, as I've said, exactly in alignment. But we need to know the theoretical picture because it actually did affect the practice; and the practice actually did, occasionally, affect the theory.

My question—where did the Elizabethan idea of genres come from?—can be misleading if it implies that there is a single source or origin. Ben Jonson was a scholar and did his primary research, so we can trace the classical sources of his comments on the kinds of drama. Shakespeare read some of what Jonson read, but the genre-theory he knew was disseminated in much the way modern theories are. Some modern critics can talk about deconstruction without having read Derrida, or Marxist literary theory without Marx, and they do not have to worry—too much—about faking it. Ideas circulate in odd ways; by the time you or I get an idea it may have gone through many foreign exchanges, been laundered and put to so many uses that looking for its origin is like looking for the origin of the money circulating through the air of electronic banking.

With regard to theories of genre, the question of origins is especially difficult. Chronologically, we can find the usual suspect, Aristotle, behind the entire structure of genre-theory and the decorum of kinds—but distantly, often more as a cultural rumour than a fact. It was not until the mid-sixteenth century that Aristotle's *Poetics* became very prominent as a direct source of ideas in early-modern European thought. The Roman poet Horace, though he wrote much later, got there first, through the wide dissemination and prestige of his *Art of Poetry*. But for the Renaissance, a rule of thumb was that the more classics the better; and if one classical source seemed to disagree with another, then the best thing to do would be interpret them until they were made to agree. The picture on Jonson's title-page is based mainly on Horace, but Horace himself drew liberally on Aristotle; and Jonson, in the collection of critical observations called *Discoveries*, shows that he knows Aristotle at first hand. We can try to sort out the elements that come from one or the other; but the actual picture that emerged for Shakespeare and his contemporaries was a palimpsest, with the one author and his traditions overwritten upon the other, and both of them overwritten by later interpreters.

Aristotle writes as a rigorous philosopher, but in the form we have it the *Poetics* seems like a set of notes (possibly his lecture notes) rather than a completely polished treatise. The result is that, for all Aristotle's rigour, later critics had plenty of opportunity to embellish and interpret. Aristotle defines poetry as an art of imitation (*mimesis*), and distinguishes various kinds of poetry by their means of imitation: a poet may speak in his own voice (lyric, and what we would call first-person narration), or partly in his own voice and partly in the voices of his characters (epic, and what would become the novel), or exclusively in the voices of his characters (drama). When it comes to drama, which is his main subject, Aristotle deals almost exclusively with tragedy—so much that later critics assumed he must have written a (now lost) complementary treatise about comedy.

Horace's *Art of Poetry*, by contrast, is written in the form of a witty personal letter to an aspiring poet. Horace is more concerned with practical advice and value judgements than is Aristotle. His theory of genre is really a compendium of advice about good writing. He advocates an ideal which came to be known as decorum: the idea that for each kind of writing there is an appropriate subject matter and style. Some things just naturally lend themselves to comedy and the comic style, some things to tragedy and the tragic style; and bad writing is writing that mixes them up. A place for everything and everything in its appropriate place: this is the watchword of decorum quoted on the Jonson title-page. Horace does not attempt to be as philosophically precise or all-embracing as Aristotle, yet his genial epistle could be read as more, rather than less, prescriptive than Aristotle.

In their discussions of plot—what Aristotle calls 'the imitation of an action'—both Aristotle and Horace stress an ideal of complex unity. Tragedy, says Aristotle, is 'the imitation of a complete and whole action of a proper magnitude'. The 'complete and whole action' involves a reversal of fortune (*peripeteia*); the best reversal is coincident with the moment of discovery or recognition (*anagnorisis*); and the 'proper magnitude' is whatever is required to bring the characters and the audience through the reversal and recognition to a sense of appropriate, necessary, even inevitable closure. In tragedy the reversal tends to be from good fortune to bad, and in comedy from bad to good. But in all imaginative writing, whether epic or drama, tragedy or comedy, unity—that is to say, completion and wholeness—is the main thing. For Aristotle, poetic unity is in a sense more organic than the unity of real life: the whole biography of an individual, imitated on stage, would not give us a sense of formal wholeness, 'for in some of the many and infinitely varied things that happen to any one person, there is no unity';[19] those 'varied things' belong to one person but not to one action or plot. A tragedy ends, not because the actors stop talking, but because the action has completed itself, and only that which has a unity of self-identity can be so completed. The parts of the work must all grow together, so much that 'if any one part is transposed or removed, the whole will be disordered and disunified'. Watching the tragic plot's moment-by-moment achievement of its final form allows the audience a cognitive and emotional satisfaction; and that satisfaction helps explain why the imitation of sad or horrible events, which would be intolerable under other circumstances, can become part of tragedy's complex pleasure.

Horace, too, stresses the artistic virtue of self-consistency, but less as a philosophical ideal of unity than as a rule for successful writing. Whether you're writing epics or plays, don't start at the beginning of the whole story, with the hero's birth, but hurry your readers right into the middle of things, leaving out whatever you can't handle, and blend it all together so that the middle isn't discordant from the end, or the end from the middle.

Aristotle and Horace agree that a play should have a beginning, a middle, and an end: the proposition invites a sceptical shrug: Do critics get famous for saying stuff like that? In fact, the underlying assumption that the poet or playwright can construct out of the most complex materials a sense of underlying order is fundamental to the idea of genres as something more than arbitrary categories. The successful work hangs together, but different works hang together differently. The plot of comedy or tragedy produces a certain kind of effect, and that is one way to know that it is unified and belongs in the same genre as other works that produce a similar effect.

But when the ideal of unity becomes too mechanical, and when the means to achieving unity become more prominent than the achievement itself, we have an idea of genre which is not only too obvious but potentially stultifying. The theory of genre then becomes prescriptive rather than descriptive, a matter of rules observed rather than similarities discovered. That danger would become real in the later seventeenth century when the ideal of unity, which could be achieved in many different ways, threatened to become a doctrine of specific technical *unities*, which had to be maintained in specific ways. Aristotle observes, on the basis of the actual plays he knows, that 'tragedy [unlike epic] attempts, as far as possible, to remain within one circuit of the sun or, at least, not depart from this by much'.[20] Horace says nothing about the amount of time that a plot (tragic or otherwise) should encompass, only that it should not put too much strain on the reader's or audience's sense of credulity. As later commentators worked on these two ideas—Aristotle's that tragedies tend to imitate briefer periods of time than epics, and Horace's that dramatic plots should have a unity of tone and purpose, and be believable—they merged into a 'precept' (as Sir Philip Sidney calls it) that the 'uttermost time' of a true tragic plot should be one day. And Sidney cites a related 'precept', that the stage should represent only a single place. Sidney is amusingly scornful of plays which violate these unities; most of Shakespeare's plays, had Sidney known them, would have been perfect targets for his scorn. Ben Jonson also cites the one-day rule, but he more clearly subordinates it to the larger ideal of dramatic wholeness: 'it behooves the action in tragedy or comedy to be let grow, till the necessity ask a conclusion, wherein two things are to be considered: first, that it exceed not the compass of one day; next, that there be left place for digression and art.'[21]

Shakespeare, like most of his theatrical contemporaries, left plenty of space for digression, even for multiple plots. The so-called unities of time and place are largely irrelevant to his plays in any of the genres. In Shakespearian tragedy, a unity of effect may be found in a plot which asks us to imagine ourselves in Venice in one scene and on Cyprus the next, or in one which moves from castle to heath to hovel to 'fields near Dover', or in one which oscillates with almost dizzying rapidity between Egypt and Rome. Occasionally Shakespeare and his contemporaries did try to observe the 'unities' in their work—but more so in comedy than tragedy. Jonson did it to hilarious effect in *Volpone*, *The Alchemist*, and other comedies built on the principle that the greatest number of mistakes crammed into the shortest time and smallest place will produce the biggest comic bang. Shakespeare himself did it only twice, at the beginning and the end of his comic career, in *The Comedy of Errors* and *The Tempest*. But by the end of the seventeenth century these so-called Aristotelian unities of time and place could look to some critics like natural, irrefutable facts of aesthetic life: as Pope put it, 'Learn hence for ancient rules a just esteem; | To copy nature is to copy them'.[22] But for Shakespeare, the unities were not rules nor were they natural; they were one set of techniques among many other ways to achieve the effect of dramatic wholeness.

Some of Aristotle's comments are bound to the circumstances of his own culture and suffer in the translation to another. According to Aristotle, we differentiate comedy from tragedy on the basis of the objects they imitate: comedy 'takes as its goal the representation of men as worse, [tragedy] as better, than the norm'. 'Tragedy is an imitation of the nobler sort of men' while 'comedy is an imitation of baser men'; such men are 'ridiculous' because of 'some error or ugliness that is painless and has no harmful effects'.[23] Out of such hints grows the Renaissance critic's demand that English tragedy should stick to 'majestical matters' (having to do, that is, with kings and other great rulers of states) and comedy should stick to clownish matters (having to do with people of low social status). A distinction based on Greek ideas of moral and social values has been translated into the social and, specifically, class terms of an entirely different culture. The aesthetic judgement performs political work, as tragedy, the noble genre, becomes associated with a conservative early-modern idea of aristocracy and monarchy.

The most influential of Aristotelian ideas about tragedy are so specific to Athenian culture that we still call them by their Greek names. Aristotle says that tragedy 'achieves, through the representation of pitiable and fearful incidents, the catharsis of such pitiable and fearful incidents'.[24] Translators have tried desperately to find an equivalent for that mysterious 'catharsis'. Maybe it means purification? Or maybe purgation?[25] But how does a play either purify or purge pity and fear by representing incidents which excite those emotions? Why do they need purifying or purging in any event? And where does all this purifying or purging take place? According to the translation I quoted above, it is in the 'incidents' of the plot itself. But most critics have assumed that catharsis is something that happens to the audience. That is the version John Milton gives in his Preface to *Samson Agonistes* (published 1671): 'Tragedy, as it was anciently composed, hath been ever held the gravest and most profitable of all other poems; therefore said by Aristotle to be of power, by raising pity and fear, or terror, to purge the mind of those and such like passions—that is, to temper and reduce them to just measure and a kind of delight, stirred up by reading or seeing those passions well imitated.' For Milton catharsis is a way of achieving emotional balance. But whatever it is and wherever it happens, the elusive idea of catharsis contributes to the sense that 'right' tragedy is a very exclusive category: many things make us laugh but few can both raise and purge the passions of pity and fear.

Clearly Shakespeare knew about the Aristotelian idea of catharsis. In *King Lear* the dead bodies of Goneril and Regan are brought on stage. The Duke of Albany is very precise, almost pedantic in his response: 'This judgement of the heavens, that makes us tremble, | Touches us not with pity' (F, 5. 3. 206–7). The death of the cruel daughters produces fear ('makes us tremble') at the spectacle of divine justice, but because it is just (the evil characters got what they deserved) it does not produce pity. The tragedy has not yet reached its 'promised end', the death of Lear bearing the body of the dead Cordelia.

If tragedy is to produce a catharsis, says Aristotle, the plot should not represent an entirely good person coming to harm nor an entirely bad person coming to good, for either situation would be too shocking or repellent to produce pity and fear; nor should it represent an entirely bad person coming to harm, for that would produce fear without pity (Albany's scenario). What is left is 'a person who is neither perfect in virtue and justice, nor one who falls into misfortune through vice and depravity; but rather, one who succumbs through' what Aristotle calls *hamartia*. Again, a key term in the critical tradition is susceptible to significantly different interpretations. The most drastic swerve in the word's history came from its use in the Greek New Testament to mean the equivalent of English 'sin'. 'Sin' belongs to the Christian tradition, not to classical Greece. In Aristotle, the *hamartia* which he associates with tragedy need imply very little in the way of moral, to say nothing of spiritual, culpability. A modern translator makes the phrase mean that the tragic character falls 'through some miscalculation'; another calls it a 'mistake'; but a Victorian translator rendered it as 'some error or frailty'.[26] The more recent interpretations suggest that *hamartia* is almost an accident such as anyone might have, while the idea of 'frailty' suggests that it is an aspect of a particular character or personality, a psychological failure. The question is how much blame to assign, and where to assign it. And that question brings the literary-critical side of things directly into contact with the moral and religious; it touches people's deepest sense of what is just or unjust, not only in plays but in the universe they represent. Bad things happen to reasonably good people. Is that because reasonably good is not good enough, as Edgar in *King Lear* believes: 'The gods are just, and of our pleasant vices | Make instruments to plague us' (F, 5. 3. 161–2)? Or is goodness irrelevant in what seems to his father Gloucester to be an amoral universe: 'As flies to wanton boys are we to th' gods; | They kill us for their sport' (F, 4. 1. 37–8)? Aristotle's word *hamartia* indicates that the tragic figure does something which contributes to his misfortune. Is that something as morally neutral as a 'mistake' or does it shade into what the Victorian translator calls, with a slightly moralizing touch, 'error or frailty', or should it even be marked with the Christian notion of 'sin'?

Because Aristotle's *Poetics* deals mainly with tragedy, it was left for later critics—the so-called grammarians or scholastics of the early

Christian and medieval eras—to supply the comic theory he neglected. The most influential of these was Donatus (fourth century AD), whose treatise on comedy was often printed and studied along with the comedies of the Roman playwright Terence. Shakespeare would have read Donatus when he was learning Latin in his Stratford grammar school. Parts of the treatise merely repeat the amalgamated views of Aristotle and Horace. From their hints Donatus supplies a history and genealogy for comedy. In this version, tragedy is the older form and comedy a more recent development. Donatus knows this because tragedy supposedly deals with more primitive actions and emotions than comedy: 'For just as man progressed, little by little, from uncouth and wild manners to gentleness, and cities were founded, and life became milder and more leisurely, so analogously the tragic mode was discovered long before the comic.'[27] The development of comedy, then, is a measure of the development of settled civilization. The original or so-called Old Comedy began as a song, not a play, sung by a chorus around a flaming altar. (This is the scene Jonson presents on his title-page to represent the birth of comedy.) Eventually actors and parts were added; but the subject matter of Old Comedy remained tied to actual events in the contemporary world and included 'the naming of citizens, who were freely described'. From this potentially scandalous type of play, satire developed as a distinct form, while comedy itself was re-formed into the so-called New Comedy. Instead of the particular, New Comedy dealt with the general or universal; it dealt with ordinary characters of 'moderate means'; and instead of bitterness it produced healthy entertainment. When comedy reached its full development, it supposedly distinguished itself from tragedy in the following schematic way:

In comedy the fortunes of men are ordinary, the onslaughts of difficulty minor, the outcomes of actions happy. But in tragedy everything is the opposite: the characters are outstanding, the fears great, the outcomes disastrous. Then again, in comedy the beginning is stormy, the end calm, but in tragedy the opposite holds true. In tragedy life is portrayed which one must flee, in comedy a life which one ought to seek. Finally, all comedy deals with fictional plots, whereas tragedy is often sought in historical reality.

The notion of comedy as a kind of equal and opposite reaction to tragedy is firmly planted in Donatus's summary. Other parts of the treatise fix the notion that comedy is a didactic form, gently teaching its audience by example what to avoid and what to embrace. Comedy does this by imitating not distinctive individual characters but types— the young lover, the bragging soldier, the doting old man, and so on. Donatus attributes to Cicero the definition of comedy as 'an imitation of life, a mirror of experience, an image of truth'. But 'life', 'experience', and 'truth' here mean the typical (and therefore, supposedly, always applicable) rather than the distinctive. Shakespeare and his contemporaries knew the theory of didactic comedy and of comic types. George Whetstone, in the Prologue to *Promos and Cassandra* (1578), gives a good summary of received opinion about how comedies should work: 'grave old men should instruct: young men should show the imperfections of youth: strumpets should be lascivious: boys unhappy: and clowns, should speak disorderly: intermingling all these actions, in such sort, as the grave matter may instruct: and the pleasant, delight.'[28] In *As You Like It*, Shakespeare creates a type, Jaques the malcontent, who sketches a brilliant catalogue of types, each of them played successively by one person in the seven ages of his life.

But knowing a type from an individual isn't always easy. Each one of us is both type and individual, the difference residing not in ourselves but in the eyes of our beholders. And it is hard to square the idea that comedy imitates ordinary folks doing ordinary things with the extraordinary characters—identical twins of opposite sexes, a man with the head of an ass—in the sometimes literally enchanted settings of Shakespearian comedy. We can notice that the very titles of the plays suggest some agreement between Shakespeare and the received version of classical genre theory: *Hamlet, Othello, King Lear, Macbeth* take their names from the distinct, irreplaceable individuals who are at the centres of their tragedies; *As You Like It, Much Ado About Nothing, A Midsummer Night's Dream, Twelfth Night* name occasions or situations which embrace all character-types equally. But the simple division into comic generality and tragic particularity, comic geniality and tragic passion, even comic happiness and tragic sorrow is only the starting point for Shakespeare's complex interrogations of the genres. In the next chapter we'll concentrate less on theories about the kinds of drama and more on the actual practice of Shakespeare and his fellow playwrights.

The Genres Staged

WE know what the genres looked like to one theoretically inclined playwright: on Ben Jonson's title-page, Comedy and Tragedy stand decorously apart, in their assigned places, paired with their adjuncts, pastoral poetry and satire. What would the genres look—and sound—like, not frozen on the expensive and exclusive page, but on the popular and often rowdy stage? One answer is found in the induction—a dramatized introduction—to a play called *A Warning for Fair Women*, performed by Shakespeare's company, the Lord Chamberlain's Men, in 1599. The anonymous author stages an argument in which the personified female figures of Comedy, History, and Tragedy bicker over who will get to put on today's play. The play itself isn't particularly interesting, but the territorial squabble over genre-rights is. We notice, for instance, that the author of *A Warning for Fair Women* divides the theatrical realm into three genres, as Heminges and Condell would do seventeen years later in organizing the Shakespeare Folio. The reason probably has less to do with theory than with box office. In the early 1590s, the Chamberlain's Men had done well with Shakespeare's first group of plays based on English history, culminating in *Richard III*. A few years later came *Richard II*, the two parts of *Henry IV*, and, in the same year as *A Warning for Fair Women*, *Henry V*. History's claim to be a genre equal to Comedy and Tragedy was of recent and very local origin: History gets onto the stage of *A Warning for Fair Women* because Shakespeare's success put her there.

The three figures carry the appropriately distinguishing signs. History enters with a drum and martial banner, Tragedy a whip and a knife, Comedy a fiddle. And they make the appropriately loud noises. Tragedy complains about the banging of History's drum and the screeching of Comedy's 'cat's guts', while Comedy sarcastically cata- logues the ingredients of a typical tragic performance:

> How some damned tyrant, to obtain a crown,
> Stabs, hangs, empoisons, smothers, cutteth throats,
> And then a Chorus too comes howling in,
> And tells us of the worrying of a cat,
> Then of a filthy whining ghost,
> Lapt in some fowl sheet, or a leather pelch,
> Comes screaming in like a pig half sticked,
> And cries *Vindicta*, revenge, revenge![1]

Whatever the genre of today's play, the scene will be busy with move- ment, sound, and special effects: Comedy's cartwheels and 'filthy fiddling tricks'; History's drums and trumpets and clashing arms; Tragedy's screams and tears, and the special effects of flashing fire and smoke. (And, no doubt, carried over from the bear-baiting pit next door to the Globe Theatre, the awful sounds of bear and dogs in mortal combat, and the bloodthirsty cries of the betting crowd.)

Still, for all the hullaballoo, the decorum of genre will, supposedly, be kept both in subject and style. Comedy will deal in 'sparks of wit' and the 'slight and childish' passion of her young lovers, while Tragedy, whose business is murder and tyranny, 'must have passions that must move the soul, | Make the heart heave, and throb within the bosom, | Extorting tears out of the strictest eyes' (ll. 44–6), all in heightened language that will 'rack [torture] a thought and strain it to his form'.

As it turns out, the day belongs to Tragedy. But only for a day. Comedy knows that audiences demand variety, and that if she and History do not appear once a week, Tragedy 'will find few that will attend her here' (l. 38). But even that assurance of a healthy repertory of genres does not quite describe the actual variety of the Elizabethan stage. The audience to even the most solemn or bloodthirsty tragedy was entertained at the same performance with comic dances, or jigs. And *A Warning for Fair Women* itself—a tabloid-style tale of adultery and murder in the middle classes—scarcely matches the expectations aroused by its induction.

As *A Warning for Fair Women* shows, Elizabethan playwrights thought in terms of the traditions of genre, and produced plays that varied and mixed rather than strictly carried out those traditions. In this chapter we'll be concerned with Shakespeare's relationship to some of his predecessors and contemporaries on the English stage. If a genre is not a set of immutable rules but the living product of a literary tradition, then the shape of the genre is defined as much by borrowings and pointed rejections of precedent, by the ways one author imitates or subverts another, as it is by any theoretical definition. I'll discuss tragedy first and turn to comedy later; and I begin this brief exercise in intertextual relations by looking at one of the most exuberantly bad (and popular) plays ever written, the *Tragedy of Cambyses, King of Persia.*

In *1 Henry IV*, Prince Hal and Falstaff, preparing for the delinquent Prince's long-delayed interview with his father, take turns playing the part of a king. Falstaff goes first. A bar-room stool becomes his royal throne, a dagger his sceptre, a cushion his crown; and he asks for 'a cup of sack to make my eyes look red, that it may be thought I have wept; for I must speak in passion, and I will do it in King Cambyses' vein' (2. 5. 387–90). Falstaff refers to a popular play from the time of Shakespeare's own youth. The flavour of it comes through vividly from its title-page: *A Lamentable Tragedy, Mixed Full of Pleasant Mirth, Containing the Life of Cambyses, King of Persia, From the beginning of his kingdom unto his death, his one good deed of execution, after that many wicked deeds and tyrannous murders committed by and through him, and last of all his odious death by God's justice appointed.* Among Cambyses' 'wicked deeds' is the one Falstaff alludes to. A good counsellor tells Cambyses that he shouldn't drink so much. Cambyses orders the counsellor to place his son before him, takes up his bow and arrow, and shoots the boy through the heart. Could a drunkard do that? Lamentable indeed. And full of pleasant mirth for anyone who thinks that each style should decently keep the generic place allotted to it. Shakespeare had already made fun of *Cambyses'* extravagant lack of decorum in the play-within-the-play of *A Midsummer Night's Dream*, with its 'very tragical mirth'. Tragical mirth may be, as Theseus objects, a contradiction in terms, but it was not uncommon on the stage Shakespeare inherited from his predecessors.

Cambyses is an entertaining monstrosity from both the Aristotelian and the Horatian points of view. Aristotle recommends a unity of action, joining a necessary beginning to a necessary middle to a virtually inevitable end. Horace tells the poet to stick to the story's main point, getting right to the middle of its matter, and leaving out whatever can't be fitted into a unified plot in which the beginning, the middle, and the end are all of a piece. *Cambyses*, by contrast, wears its episodic quality proudly on its title-page: the aesthetic principle of organization is almost literally one-damn-thing-after-another, until the playwright and God decide they've had enough. The stage direction reads 'Enter the King, without a gown, a sword thrust up into his side, bleeding'; and, with rhyme but little reason, Cambyses dies a protracted if morally justified death:

> Out, alas! What shall I do? My life is finishèd.
> Wounded I am by sudden chance, my blood is minishèd.
>
> .   .   .   .   .
>
> Who but I in such a wise his death's wound could have got?
> As I on horseback up did leap, my sword from scabbard shot
> And ran me thus into my side, as you right well may see.
> A marvels chance unfortunate that in this wise should be.
> I feel myself a-dying now; of life bereft am I;
> And Death hath caught me with his dart; for want of blood I spy.
> Thus, gasping, here on ground I lie; for nothing I do care.
> A just reward for my misdeeds my death doth plain declare.[2]

Shakespeare's parody can't surpass this. Still, *Cambyses* is worth pausing over for a moment more, since both its excesses and its virtues—the two, as in most cases they are, tightly entwined—predict the excesses and virtues of much greater plays. Of 'Pyramus and Thisbe' Theseus asks, 'How shall we find the concord of this discord?' It is a question we have to ask about many of Shakespeare's own plays, in each of the genres.

The printed text of *Cambyses* includes a list of characters divided so that an acting company of eight men could, by doubling parts, play all thirty-eight roles. This was standard operating procedure on the Elizabethan stage: Shakespeare, too, had to keep in mind his company's limited personnel as he wrote. What we notice about *Cambyses'* character-list is not only the actors' virtuosity in playing as many as seven different parts, but the extraordinary range in the *kinds* of parts.

One actor plays the part of 'Counsel', a character whose name is also his moral function. The next time the actor appears, he plays 'Huf': like his pals Ruf and Snuf, he is a comic type-character. The same actor plays Praxaspes, the unfortunate counsellor who advises Cambyses to give up drinking: we recognize him as a kind of historical character (whether he ever existed off-stage or not), more individuated than Counsel or Huf, and distantly approaching what modern readers might think of as a realistic character. But in the same play, an actor plays the mythological Venus and another plays Cupid.

The issue of characterization—of how Shakespeare chooses to represent the agents of his plots—is inseparable from the issue of genre. Literary historians sometimes call a play like *Cambyses* a 'mixed morality', referring to an older, more strictly allegorical sort of morality play, like the fifteenth-century *Everyman*, which has become mixed up, as it were, with other modes of representation. The genres provide materials and impose meaningful restraints and possibilities for characterization. A character in comedy can get hit and hit again and bounce up none the worse for wear, because the genre gives the character an immunity from harm that the characters in tragedy notably lack. A tragic character, like Hamlet, can search within himself for that which passes show, creating the illusion of psychic depth, of a psychological distinctiveness which is simultaneously his privilege and frailty; the comic character tends to lack such interiority in proportion to his possession of immunity from psychic harm. But in *Cambyses* there seems little reason why comically immune characters like Huf, Ruf, and Snuf inhabit the same stage as Praxaspes or his poor doomed son. And Shakespeare, too, rather than strictly purging the helter-skelter excesses of the mixed-morality, at times enthusiastically embraces his lawless legacy; but he does so in ways which also reflect upon that legacy with sophisticated self-consciousness. Antipholus of Syracuse, in *The Comedy of Errors*, enters the play as if he were a character in tragedy, soliloquizing about his psychic peril. He cannot find contentment in this world where, in his search for the necessary others who give him his identity, he confounds himself, like a drop of water fallen into the great ocean: 'So I, to find a mother and a brother, | In quest of them, unhappy, lose myself' (1. 2. 39–40). Enter, immediately, the wrong twin-servant, and so begins the spiralling tower of comic errors. Antipholus may want to be a tragic hero, full of hidden depths, but the genre won't allow it. In later comedies, including all the so-called problem comedies, there can be considerable tension between a character's assumption of a Hamlet-like interiorized individuality and the comic plot's determination to move that character to the inclusive ending. The romances, Shakespeare's last plays, are also his grandest experiments in mixed genres and mixed or compound characters.

Shakespearian Tragedy in Context

It could have been otherwise. In tragedy, for instance, Shakespeare might have followed the example recommended by Sir Philip Sidney. For that learned gentleman, the idea of tragedy raised such high expectations that most actual tragedies were a disappointment. His *Apology for Poetry*, written in the early 1580s, is an eloquent defence of the literary imagination; but when it comes to English drama, Sidney finds more to attack than defend. He cannot cite a single English play which can stand 'as an exact model of all Tragedies'. We've already glanced at his complaint that English playwrights muddle the generic boundaries. They cross-breed a 'mongrel tragicomedy', which yields neither the 'admiration and commiseration' of tragedy nor 'the right sportfulness' of comedy. They 'thrust in clowns by head and shoulders to play a part in majestical matters', so that 'all their plays be neither right tragedies nor right comedies'.[3]

But at least there was *Gorboduc* (1561–2), the one English tragedy Sidney *almost* approved of: it is 'full of stately speeches and well sounding phrases ... and as full of notable morality'[4]—even if it does screw up the unities of place and time. *Gorboduc* was collaboratively written by two aristocrats, Sir Thomas Sackville and Thomas Norton, to be performed before an audience of nobility. It is made up of five acts, as Horace prescribed. It employs a Chorus, another sanctioned element. It mixes no clowns with its kings: no one would ever accuse *Gorboduc* of an indecorous descent into comedy. And it keeps to its main point rigorously and repeatedly. No doubt its political content kept the original spectators, including Queen Elizabeth, on the edge of their courtly seats. Each act begins with a dumb show and ends with a Chorus, all to make clear the meaning of the intervening action, that monarchs should maintain a unified kingdom. And they certainly should not divide that kingdom between their children, as foolish King Gorboduc did. The ostensible similarity between *Gorboduc* and *King Lear*—also a tragedy about a king who divides his kingdom—mainly serves to underscore the vast difference. For instance, Gorboduc begins a Lear-like rant about his rebellious son: 'O heavens, send down the flames of your revenge! | Destroy, I say, with flash of wreakful fire | The traitor son and then the wretched sire!' but his anger is quickly contained by the moralizing Chorus, who comes on to tell us, blandly, that 'the lust of kingdom knows no sacred faith' and can turn child against parent, brother against brother.[5] *King Lear* may include the same commonplace, but neither the play nor its massively demanding central character can be pacified with a political slogan. The advice to monarchs is contained in *King Lear*, but the play is not contained by the conservative advice.

Still, a play like *Gorboduc*, written for court in the early years of Elizabeth's reign, helps us bring to the foreground an historical context of Shakespeare's own tragedies. From the early *Titus Andronicus* and *Richard III* to *Macbeth* and *Antony and Cleopatra*, Shakespearian tragedy deals with 'majestical matters' not only because genre theorists said it should but because the actions of real majesty—Queen Elizabeth or King James—were of immediate concern to many in Shakespeare's audience, and of life-and-death concern to some. Courtiers under both Elizabeth and James had to distinguish themselves; to earn royal favour they had to perform daring military or diplomatic actions, and display their own magnificence in acts of conspicuous expenditure. Do it too well, however, and the outstanding courtier could become a threat to the monarch his acts were designed to please. The peace of the realm depended on a careful balancing act between the powers of sovereign and nobility. And in the late years of Queen Elizabeth's reign, with no heir-apparent clearly in sight, the nation itself could seem as threatened with disintegration as did the ageing body of the queen. The beginning of King James's reign marked the temporary weathering but by no means the end of the political crisis which raged until one of Shakespeare's great tragic themes, the killing of a king, was enacted upon the body of a very real King Charles I. *Julius Caesar*, *Antony and Cleopatra*, and *Coriolanus* are so-called 'Roman plays', but they are very English in staging the conflict between the singularly remarkable individual and the demands of the political realm. *Titus*

Andronicus, *Richard II*, *Julius Caesar*, *Macbeth*, and *King Lear* are not, like *Gorboduc*, didactic warnings about the evils of ambition and the pitfalls of royal succession, but their deeply troubled engagement with issues of inheritance and legitimacy is a product of the troubled times. *Hamlet* strikes us as 'timeless' because its rhetorical richness responds endlessly to the concerns of successive audiences, but *Hamlet* is also a late sixteenth-century play of state, about the anxiety of uncertain rule and the passage of power from one generation to the next; and as much as the earlier *Gorboduc* it (like *Macbeth* and *King Lear*, or the Roman plays or the English chronicle history plays) owes many of its definitive characteristics to the time's political obsessions.

Philip Sidney admired *Gorboduc*'s poetry; it climbed, he said, 'to the height of Seneca's style'. Seneca (*c*.4 BC–AD 65), the Roman philosopher and poet, wrote Latin tragedies (probably not meant for stage performance) on Greek themes. Shakespeare may have read them in their recent English translations. His theatrical contemporaries certainly did. A fascinating bit of evidence links Seneca to a play called *Hamlet* which Shakespeare did *not* write, but which is related to the later *Hamlet* he did write. In 1589, Thomas Nashe wrote a preface to his friend Robert Greene's prose romance *Menaphon*, satirizing a whole host of (as he saw them) contemporary literary absurdities. He criticized 'our trivial translators', offering in the process this back-handed compliment: 'English *Seneca* read by candlelight yields many good sentences, as *Blood is a beggar*, and so forth: and if you entreat him fair in a frosty morning, he will afford you whole *Hamlets*, I should say handfuls of tragical speeches. . . . [But] *Seneca* let blood line by line and page by page, at length must needs die to our stage.'[6] According to Nashe, the quick and easy way to write whole *Hamlets*-ful of tragedies was to drain the translations of Seneca's bloody lines onto your own page. But you'd better do it quickly, he implies, because the fashion won't last long.

Seneca's style is declamatory and self-consciously rhetorical; his characters speak lengthily, punctuating their philosophical complaints with pithier aphorisms, of the 'Blood is a beggar' sort. In the twentieth century, T. S. Eliot wrote that Seneca was less a consistent moralist than a poet of 'postures': 'The posture which gives the greatest opportunity for effect, hence for the Senecan morality, is the posture of dying: death gives his characters the opportunity for their most sententious aphorisms—a hint which Elizabethan dramatists were only too ready to follow.'[7] The ingenious rhetoric of tragic death, the zingy one-liners with which villains and heroes alike expire, is one of several features the sixteenth- and seventeenth-century stage owed, if indirectly, to the example of 'English Seneca'.

English attempts at Senecan style deserve some of the praise, and blame, for the occasionally over-the-top rhetoric, the presence of trouble-making ghosts and other paranormal phenomena, and the emphasis on bloody deaths by spectacularly ingenious means which characterize one strand of English tragedy. But in Seneca, physical atrocities are not staged but described by a Chorus or Messenger; English playwrights brought those horrors right onto the stage. Such notorious moments as Gloucester's blinding in *King Lear* or the self-mutilation of Hieronimo (who bites out his own tongue) in Thomas Kyd's *The Spanish Tragedy* are Senecan in spirit but distinctly English in practice. Shakespeare's relation to Seneca is indirect; as T. S. Eliot nicely puts it, 'by the time that *The Spanish Tragedy* and the old *Hamlet* had made their success, the English playwright was under the influence of Seneca by being under the influence of his own predecessors.'[8] Shakespeare's earliest tragedy, *Titus Andronicus*, was more highly regarded by its first audiences than it has been since, partly because those audiences found some of its more extravagant elements—a mother, for instance, mistakenly eats her own sons baked in a pie, a variation on a theme in Seneca's *Thyestes*—to be the height of fashion. Contemporary Senecanism may have been a youthful enthusiasm for Shakespeare, one of those blind academic alleys, like *Gorboduc*, which he did not ultimately make his highway. But he never fully turned away from it. When Hamlet asks the players at Elsinore to give him a taste of their quality, he asks for a play he once heard—not a play to please the multitude, for ''twas caviar to the general': it is a Senecan play about Pyrrhus, Priam, and Hecuba, and Shakespeare's pastiche displays his critical self-consciousness of the style.

The impulse of 'English Seneca' is still very much alive in the work of Shakespeare's younger contemporary John Webster. But Webster's Seneca is mediated through the even stronger influence of Shakespeare himself. Webster's *The White Devil* was a failure at its first performance. In the printed version, Webster defends his play. He acknowledges ('if it be objected that it is no true dramatic poem') that the play fails to observe 'all the critical rules, as of height of style, and gravity of person.... sententious *Chorus*, and... weighty *Nuntius* [messenger]'.[9] But Webster also knows that only a small, learned minority objected to his failure to observe a strict Senecan manner. Webster blames his play's failure not on his own falling off but on 'the breath that comes from the uncapable multitude', which would still have poisoned the play's reception even if he had thrown classically correct pearls before the theatre-going swine. What's interesting about the episode for our purpose is the tension Webster expresses between his concern for theoretical correctness, on the Senecan pattern, and his equal interest in being successful in a theatre that wanted blood-and-guts at least as much as it wanted high-sounding tragic speeches.

The courtly and academic *Gorboduc*, the learned vogue for Seneca: these represent possibilities for tragedy which Shakespeare did not reject but transformed in his own mature tragedies. Other antecedents were similarly turned and twisted as they entered the fabric of Shakespeare's tragedies. One of these belonged more to the page than to the stage. In Chaucer's *Canterbury Tales* the Monk is asked to take his turn as storyteller. Nothing could be easier: he'll tell 'tragedies'. Tragedies, he says, are stories about people who stood in great prosperity, fell out of high degree into misery, and ended wretchedly. They are stories *De Casibus virorum illustrium*: concerning the fall of illustrious men. Sometimes, he says, they are in verse, sometimes in prose; drama is not part of his definition. The Monk begins his anthology of dismal stories with Lucifer, who fell from heaven's high degree to hell; goes on to Adam, who also fell from prosperity to 'mischance'; then Sampson (ditto), Hercules (ditto), Nebuchadnezzar, Balthasar, Queen Cenobia (women, too, can fall from high degree and end in misery), Julius Caesar, Nero, Cresus. And he could go on forever, each tale telling the same tale, each demonstrating the inevitably 'tragic' effects of 'Fortune': first you go up, then you come down. But his listeners rebel: a little of this dismally repetitive stuff goes a long way. The Knight wants to hear 'gladsome' stories. The Host also has had more than enough of Fortune and Tragedy: to 'hear of heaviness', he says, is a pain.

Chaucer's Monk's tales are parodies of the *De Casibus* stories which contributed one strand to the complex of ideas and forms which were being called tragedy in Shakespeare's time. Boccaccio (1313–75) began the fashion for such collections. The most important English version is *The Mirror for Magistrates* (1559, with many subsequent, enlarged editions), written by various authors including Sir Thomas Sackville, the co-author of *Gorboduc*. It is a collection of first-person verse narratives spoken by famous men and women, many of them figures from English history. *The Mirror for Magistrates* historicized and politicized the *De casibus* form; by looking in this tragic glass, rulers and other players of the political game would learn lessons, not only about Fortune in general, but about English history and what it could imply about contemporary politics. Shakespeare knew *The Mirror for Magistrates*. It influenced his choice of subjects and treatment in both his histories and tragedies. But he also transformed what he inherited, by giving a new complexity to the plot that runs uphill towards success and declines to a miserable death. No longer, in Shakespeare's tragedies, does this plot teach a simple lesson about the inevitable way of a world governed by fickle Fortune.

The so-called subplot of *King Lear* encapsulates a brilliant shard of the old *De casibus* pattern. Edgar, the legitimate heir to the Earl of Gloucester, falls from his inherited social height until he must take upon himself 'the basest and most poorest shape | That ever penury in contempt of man | Brought near to beast' (F, 2. 2. 170–2). In his abject disguise as the mad beggar, Poor Tom, he meets his own father, blind, bleeding, and in despair: another great man fallen. And the madman leads the blindman to the indefinite stage-space which editors sometimes localize as 'fields near Dover'. There Edgar and Gloucester climb a hill of their own imaginative creation. They stand at 'th'extreme verge', and from 'the dread summit of this chalky bourne' Gloucester 'down precipitat[es]' to end his 'wretchedness ... by death' (F, 4. 5. 1–79). But there was no cliff, and the literalized fall of this great man is a pratfall. The moment hovers between horror and absurdity. 'Thy life's a miracle', says the disguised Edgar; 'look up', he tells his blind father, and 'Think that the clearest gods, who make them honours | Of men's impossibilities, have preserved thee' (F, 4. 5. 73–4). Almost immediately after, the stage direction reads, 'Enter King Lear, mad', a 'side-piercing sight' which proves nothing about the justice or, for that matter, the injustice of the 'gods' but only that 'The worst is not | So long as we can say "This is the worst"' (F, 4. 1. 27–8). In *King Lear* characters go up and down, but no two characters, possibly no two members of the audience, find in that rising-and-falling action exactly the same vision. Edgar will always find in suffering the confirmation of an optimistic faith; Kent will always rebuke him: 'Vex not his ghost. O, let him pass. He hates him | That would upon the rack of this tough world | Stretch him out longer' (F, 5. 3. 289–91). All we know for a certainty is that Cordelia is 'dead as earth'; she will 'come no more. | Never, never, never, never, never' (5. 3. 236, 283–4). The faithful may have their faith confirmed, the sceptics will be hardened in their disbelief. On the simplest of narrative patterns, concerning the fall of illustrious people, Shakespeare has constructed a tragedy which makes of its final, apparently simple injunction an almost impossibly difficult burden: 'The weight of this sad time we must obey, | Speak what we feel, not what we ought to say' (F, 5. 3. 299–300). That necessity for speaking, and the difficulty of it, will be among the characteristics of the genre we will explore in this book's final chapter, when we turn to the tragedies in detail.

Tragic Characters

Something amazing happens in the third act of *3 Henry VI*: Richard, Duke of Gloucester—soon to be King Richard III—steps forward on the empty stage and, speaking about himself, creates himself, or creates the illusion of a self creating itself, with a vividness never before achieved on the English stage. The beginning of Richard's soliloquy does not yet know its end: the speech enacts a process of discovery. The question for Richard is what to do, or rather what to become, in light of his inability to do and be the things he wishes: I cannot become king, because too many legitimate claimants stand between me and the crown; I cannot 'make my heaven in a lady's lap', because 'love forswore me in my mother's womb'. Each statement of what he supposedly cannot do is infused with the vigour of a mind capable of imagining, and maybe therefore doing, anything, so that each statement of impossibility converts itself into a dramatic possibility: Richard cannot be king, but his rhetoric makes us believe he will be king; he cannot be a lover, but his rhetoric assures us he can have any woman his ambition requires. To the audience, this inventively wicked Richard gives a thrill both of foreboding and of vicarious power, as he erects each impediment in order to reveal the skill involved in overcoming it. The speech is full of back-trackings and second-thoughts—the traces of a mind listening to itself and responding. That process of self-consciousness is, for the misshapen Richard, also a process of self-torment:

> I'll make my heaven to dream upon the crown,
> And whiles I live, t'account this world but hell,
> Until my misshaped trunk that bears this head
> Be round impalèd with a glorious crown.
> And yet I know not how to get the crown.
>
> (3. 2. 168–72)

Richard announces his 'dream' of kingship, and immediately recognizes that it is *only* a dream. We witness a mind making and blocking its own desires—a process brilliantly embodied in the back-and-forth of Richard's simile:

> And I—like one lost in a thorny wood,
> That rends the thorns and is rent with the thorns,
> Seeking a way and straying from the way,
> Not knowing how to find the open air,
> But toiling desperately to find it out –
> Torment myself to catch the English crown.
>
> (174–9)

All the winding and turning of his mind against itself then gathers to a moment of sheer exuberant determination to end both physical and moral restraint: 'And from that torment will I free myself, | Or hew my way out with a bloody axe' (180–1).

The illusion of self-consciousness which Shakespeare creates for Richard in this speech is prerequisite for the achievements of all his tragic characters, whether they appear in plays that Heminges and Condell placed among the histories or the tragedies. For starkest contrast, compare Richard's declaration of purpose with that by a character in *Cambyses*. The character, Ambidexter, is a so-called Vice-figure, and he has some kinship with Richard. Like Richard, he takes the audience into his confidence; his dramatic purpose is to create mischief; his antics delight audiences despite (or because of?) his wickedness. And so he tells us: 'My name is Ambidexter. I signify one | That with both hands can play.'[10] Ambidexter's name is his nature, and what he is he always has been, always will be: that's what he 'signifies'. But Richard's relation to his own destiny, like the relation of all Shakespearian tragic characters to their destiny, is more complex. He is a *determined* character, full of purposiveness to make himself the author of his own being, the shaper of his own plot; yet he is also *determined* in the sense of being destined, doomed, a character, for all his self-willing and creative energy, who can never escape the play which contains him, the plot which traces his doom. All Shakespeare's tragic heroes and heroines, from Romeo and Juliet, who try to rewrite the destinies that are, supposedly, written in the stars, to Coriolanus, whose fatal desire is to 'stand as if a man were author of himself', are torn between their assertions of freedom and the fatality of the dramatic plot.

No predecessor or contemporary taught Shakespeare how to create this kind of tragic character. But two playwrights, Christopher Marlowe (1564–93) and Thomas Kyd (1558–94), were founding co-workers in the mode Shakespeare would later stamp his own. The chronology of composition is uncertain; the relationships among the three cannot be stated as a simple lineage of direct influences. But Marlowe's two-part *Tamburlaine* almost certainly preceded both *3 Henry VI* and *Titus Andronicus*. Its prologue announces that something new and vital has burst onto the Elizabethan stage. The theatrical self-confidence of Marlowe's spokesman presages Richard's I-can-do-anything rhetoric in *3 Henry VI*:

> From jigging veins of rhyming mother wits,
> And such conceits as clownage keeps in pay,
> We'll lead you to the stately tent of war,
> Where you shall hear the Scythian Tamburlaine
> Threat'ning the world with high astounding terms
> And scourging kingdoms with his conquering sword.
> View but his picture in this tragic glass,
> And then applaud his fortunes as you please.[11]

This mighty Marlovian verse-line, bidding its contemptuous farewell to the 'jigging vein' of a whole generation of plays like *Cambyses*, is a verbal instrument Shakespeare will play infinite variations upon in his own tragedies.

'Applaud his fortunes *as you please*': one of Marlowe's achievements was to create characters with whom members of an audience might be very differently pleased. Is Tamburlaine, the shepherd who conquers the world, a kind of cosmic scourge or merely a monster of unappeasable egotism? Tamburlaine is massively inflexible; but in other plays, Marlowe, like Shakespeare, experiments with the sinuous sound of a mind in self-creative motion. In *Edward II*—a tragedy which at several points invokes the *De casibus* mode—Piers Gaveston, the king's lover, is an attractive object of romantic desire and also a cunning social climber:

> What greater bliss can hap to Gaveston
> Than live and be the favourite of a king?
>
> .   .   .   .   .
>
> Farewell base stooping to the lordly peers.
> My knee shall bow to none but to the king.
> As for the multitude that are but sparks,
> Raked up in embers of their poverty—
> *Tanti*; I'll fawn first on the wind
> That glanceth on my lips and flieth away.
>
> (1. 1. 4–5, 18–23)

Gaveston is a character about whom we cannot make up our mind: an attractive villain, a victimizer and a victim, a political parasite and a loving friend. And in King Edward himself, to an even greater degree, Marlowe created a character at once contemptible (irresponsible, petty, selfish) and capable of inspiring the kind of sympathy which Shakespearian tragedy requires for its characters.

Marlowe's *Edward II* was an important stimulus to Shakespeare in his development as a writer of history plays: as we'll see in a later chapter, the shift in dramatic emphasis from Shakespeare's first to his second historical tetralogy probably owes much to Marlowe's example. And the complexity of audience response to Marlowe's Edward, torn as it is between moral judgement and dramatic sympathy, will also mark our response to Shakespeare's tragic characters. We watch the murderous but also self-destructive careers of Macbeth and Lady Macbeth not with loathing but with pity and fear—the emotions Aristotle associated with tragedy. Many of Shakespeare's tragic heroes and heroines are, arguably, moral monsters—if not murderers (Hamlet, Othello, Macbeth) still stunning in their selfishness (Lear), the unbendingness of their will (Coriolanus), the heedlessness of their passion (Antony and Cleopatra). With such characters, as with Marlowe's, the comforting moral certainty of the older *De casibus* pattern no longer suffices.

The Tragical History of the Life and Death of Doctor Faustus is Marlowe's most daring experiment in simultaneously invoking and subverting moral, indeed theological, certainty. There can be no doubt that Faustus is damned, as Lucifer and Mephistophilis literally bear him quick to hell. The magician, too smart for his own good, has sold his soul for worldly knowledge and purchased eternal pain. Nowhere in Shakespeare do the trappings of the medieval Christian cosmos appear as explicitly as they do in *Doctor Faustus*. But the Marlowe who dramatized a universe where good angels fight bad angels for the possession of human souls, and where the mouth of hell is a visible stage property, is also the Marlowe who (it was said) taught lessons in atheism, and claimed that 'the only beginning of religion was to keep men in awe'.[12] And in *Doctor Faustus*, in the process of staging a traditional Christian cosmos, Marlowe makes the tradition available for sceptical scrutiny. Should an audience feel contempt or admiration for the breath-taking rebelliousness that pits Faustus against God? Should we feel that Faustus only gets what he deserves? Or should we find in the unavailing terror of Faustus's final hour an implicit indictment of the God who does not save Faustus? *Doctor Faustus* has the power to unsettle the Christian verities it seems to affirm; it shows rebellion's sure punishment, and allows the possibility that the punishment itself might justify rebellion. Shakespeare, too, will experiment with a similar emotional and intellectual openness in the more secular tragic contexts of *King Lear* and *Macbeth*. The resulting complexity reinvents the genre and makes it what we call, with some injustice to Christopher Marlowe, 'Shakespearian' tragedy.

Thomas Kyd is generally assumed to have been the author of the (lost) play about *Hamlet* which preceded Shakespeare's. Little else of his work has survived, either. But what does survive, *The Spanish Tragedy*, was one of the most enduringly popular and—for Shakespeare among others— most influential plays of the entire Elizabethan era. In the Induction to *Bartholomew Fair* (1614) Ben Jonson refers to Kyd's play by its alternative title, *Hieronimo*, and pairs it with *Titus Andronicus* as the very type of an old-fashioned but still popular drama: 'He that will swear *Hieronimo* or *Andronicus* are the best plays yet... [shows that his judgement] is constant and hath stood still those five and twenty, or thirty, years.' Presumably there were enough such theatre-goers to give the joke its punch. As late as 1652 we hear 'the awful tale of a young lady who, being accustomed in health to seeing a play a day, on her death-bed continued ever crying "Oh Hieronimo, Hieronimo, methinks I see thee, brave Hieronimo" and "fixing her eyes, intentively, as if she had seen Hieronimo acted, sending out a deep sigh, she suddenly died."'[3] The dying lady's words testify, among other things, to the moral problem, not only of excessive theatre-going, but of Kyd's so-called 'revenge tragedy'. A twentieth-century scholar writes that 'there is hardly a doubt that, mad or sane, Hieronimo was a villain to the English audience'.[4] Yet the record of responses to Hieronimo suggests that there's plenty of doubt about how audiences responded to Kyd's maddened revenger.

We'll look further at revenge tragedies, like Kyd's, in Chapter 5. Here, only a few comments about the importance of Kyd's contribution. Hieronimo is Knight Marshall, a kind of chief justice, of Spain. But when Hieronimo's son, Horatio, is killed, Hieronimo is blocked in his efforts, first to find out the killers and then to get redress for his grievances. The audience knows, however, that Hieronimo will eventually get his revenge: the play opens with a character named Revenge assuring Don Andrea (whose death sets off the chain of events which leads to the murder of Hieronimo's son) that he will see 'the author of [his] death . . . Deprived of life'. *The Spanish Tragedy* is Revenge's play: 'Here sit we down to see the mystery, | And serve for Chorus in this tragedy.'[5]

Revenge's confident omniscience (the character falls asleep during parts of the action) is matched by Hieronimo's bafflement and powerlessness. Kyd constructs a situation in which the grief-stricken old father can only stumble blindly towards a conclusion that Revenge has, in effect, already scripted. In desperate pursuit of that conclusion, Hieronimo is driven to more and more extreme forms of rhetoric—words substituting for the action he cannot achieve—until he is driven to the ultimately elaborate but ineffectual speech of madness. *The Spanish Tragedy* was famous, and infamous, for its elaborately self-conscious 'Senecan' rhetoric. But Kyd isn't just showing off. His play is in a sense *about* words—and by extension about drama—and about the desperate need to find relief for great pain through adequate expression. The greater the impediment, the more elaborate the attempt to speak and find responsiveness in a world grown deaf. In the following great passage, Hieronimo uses all the art of Elizabethan rhetoric— balanced and antithetical words and phrases, repetitions, variations ('just', 'unjustly', 'justice')—to express the frustration of his need for an adequate response:

> O eyes, no eyes, but fountains fraught with tears;
> O life, no life, but lively form of death;
> O world, no world, but mass of public wrongs,
> Confus'd and fill'd with murder and misdeeds;
> O sacred heavens! If this unhallow'd deed,
> If this inhuman and barbarous attempt,
> If this incomparable murder thus
> Of mine, but now no more my son,
> Shall unreveal'd and unrevenged pass,
> How should we term your dealings to be just,
> If you unjustly deal with those that in your justice trust?
>
> Eyes, life, world, heavens, hell, night, and day,
> See, search, show, send, some man, some mean, that may—
> (3. 2. 1–23)

The symmetrical formality of the speech is at a different stylistic pole from those Shakespearian soliloquies which, with equal but more covert artistry, seem to spring from a living mind. But we'll see later how many of Shakespeare's tragic characters also enact, like Hieronimo, their frustration with the gap between words and deeds, speech and meaning. One thinks, for instance, of Hamlet, who has that within which passes show, as he watches the professional actor stage his grief for the fictitious Hecuba: 'What would he do | Had he the motive and the cue for passion | That I have?' (2. 2. 562–4)

Hieronimo finally discovers the means for revenge by staging a play within the play, becoming both 'Author and actor in this tragedy' (4. 4. 147). He writes each part in a different language: 'But this will be a mere confusion, | And hardly shall we all be understood' (4. 1. 180–1), one of his actors objects. Exactly: it is the play of Babel, of misunderstanding and solitude amidst society. Hieronimo stages it in a locked theatre, where the unknowing actors will have no escape from their roles. And with this incomprehensible script and inside that locked theatre, acting will indeed become action, as make-believe killing brings about 'real' murder, and as Hieronimo finds both his revenge and his own death in a play-within-a-play. The idea that 'all the world's a stage' was an Elizabethan commonplace. Even in *As You Like It*, the comedy where that phrase appears, it expressed a sad, if not necessarily tragic, view of life: according to Jaques, each person plays many roles, and his acts are seven ages leading inevitably to the 'last scene of all... second childishness and mere oblivion, | Sans teeth, sans eyes, sans taste, sans everything' (2. 7. 163–6). Sir Walter Ralegh's variation on the world-as-stage idea is even more pertinent to Kyd's tragedy, and to Shakespeare's tragedies and comedies:

> What is our life? A play of passion,
> Our mirth the music of division,
> Our mothers' wombs the tiring-houses be,
> Where we are dressed for this short comedy.
>
> .   .   .
>
> Thus march we playing to our latest rest,
> Only we die in earnest—that's no jest.[16]

Shakespearian Comedy in Context

Tragedy requires a theatre, even if it represents its theatre as a metaphor for human limitation. But comedy can be as big as all outdoors. It can happen anywhere, on a street corner or the back of a wagon, in an inn yard or a stately hall—wherever there's room to juggle, tumble, trade insults and jokes. Tragedy has flourished sporadically in theatrical history, but comedy is forever. A survey of the predecessors and contemporaries who helped Shakespeare rework the genre therefore has to be very limited if it is not to be endless.

The first self-consciously 'literary' comedies in English were the so-called interludes which flourished in the mid-sixteenth century. Knock-about interludes like *Ralph Roister Doister* and *Gammer Gurton's Needle* were written by scholars for scholarly audiences at Oxford, Cambridge, the Inns of Court, and the royal court itself. They rowdily challenge the often reasonable modern assumption that academic writing is by definition dull and decorous. The interludes tended in the direction of farce—towards that pole of comedy where the humour is broadest, the situations most absurd, the language most rollicking. To the post-Shakespearian reader they may seem crude. The fact that they were written for scholarly audiences doesn't guarantee that they aren't. But such audiences were likely to recognize in the best of the interludes an artful blending of English humour with plots and characters derived from the Roman plays of Plautus and Terence, written in full awareness of the critical tradition of generic decorum.

The prologue to Nicholas Udall's *Ralph Roister Doister*, for instance, promises to avoid scurrility or any 'mirth wherein is abuse':[17] Udall knows the historical distinction, passed on by Donatus, between the New Comedy of type-characters and the Old Comedy of rough personal satire. The play unobtrusively fulfils the 'unities' of place and time. And Udall follows tradition in assigning a didactic purpose not only to his own play but to its classical models. Modern audiences may not find as much 'virtuous lore' as Udall says he finds 'secretly' declared in the comedies of Plautus and Terence; he claims he is following their example in his own 'comedy, or interlude . . . Which against the vainglorious doth inveigh' (Prologue 24). Udall borrows his title character from the similar character in Plautus's *Braggart Warrior*. Roister Doister, a block-headed coward posing as a tough-guy, enter- tains the absurd belief that the lovely Dame Christian Custance would be flattered to become his (rich) bride. His double-dealing partner is Matthew Merrygreek, a character recognizable as the parasite-figure of New Comedy. But in *Roister Doister* he is simultaneously a native English character-type, a Vice-figure like Ambidexter in *Cambyses*. And throughout the play Udall gives his classical precedents an Eng- lish twist. This is not just a matter of the characters' names, Madge Mumblecrust, Tom Truepenny, and the rest. Even his rhymed, four- stress verse line translates the metrical variety and verbal ingenuity of Plautus's Latin into a thoroughly English context—for instance when Roister Doister's servant re-creates the sound of their unsuccessful wooing:

> Then up to our lute at midnight, 'twangledome twang',
> Then 'twang' to our sonnets, and 'twang' with our dumps,
> And 'heyhough' from our heart, as heavy as lead lumps;
> Then to our recorder with 'toodleloodle poop',
> As the howlet out of an ivy bush should hoop.
> Anon to our gittern, 'Thrumpledum, thrumpledum, thrum,
> Thrumpledom, thrumpledom, thrumpledom, thrum.'
>
> (2. 1. 600–6)

It's good nonsense, although no one would mistake it for Shake-speare. Yet Shakespeare was shortly to explore and exploit some of the same generic expectations and forms that the interlude uses. The climax comes in Act 4, when Dame Custance and her female friends beat Roister Doister in mock battle. The comic battle between women and men is a tradition as ancient as Aristophanes' *Lysistrata*; a gen-eration after Udall that tradition will include *The Merry Wives of Windsor* and (in Andrew Aguecheek's duelling with Cesario) *Twelfth Night*. Act 5 is taken up with the jealous suspicions of Custance's true love, Gawin Goodluck. Masculine possessive jealousy is always repre-hensible, but in drama it isn't inherently either funny or sad: the conventions of genre make it one or the other or, on rare occasions, both. Custance's not-so-hard effort to prove her innocence reveals her kinship with Shakespearian female characters we'll encounter in his comedy (Hero in *Much Ado About Nothing*), tragedy (Desdemona in *Othello*), and romances (Innogen in *Cymbeline*, Hermione in *The Win-ter's Tale*). Udall, however, leaves no doubt about his interlude's genre: Goodluck recognizes Dame Custance's constancy, Roister Doister is forgiven, and the play ends with a song and the promise of a wedding.

By the late 1580s, when Shakespeare was beginning his career, the interludes were already old-fashioned. More stylish now were plays that tended, not towards farce, but towards what we call romantic comedy. They are romantic because they deal with young love but also because, like the non-dramatic romances from which they often derived their plots, they are about a hero's or heroine's quest (often in disguise) to gain or regain an identity and find a home. Relative to farce, romantic comedies are verbally elegant. And none were more elegant than the plays of John Lyly (*c*.1554–1606).

Before Lyly turned to writing plays he was already famous as the author of the non-dramatic *Euphues: The Anatomy of Wit* (1578) and its sequel, *Euphues and his England* (1580). Those works, enormously influential in their time, are remembered now less for their content than for their prose style, a style so often imitated and parodied that it acquired its own generic name, 'Euphuism'. This is not an art that hides its artfulness. It is a style that seems almost sculpted rather than written, or perhaps put together like a mosaic of elaborately balanced and antithetical phrases, heavily marked by alliteration and internal rhyme. We recognize it as English but, compared even to the verse of the interludes, an English that is almost a foreign language. The exotic effect is carried also in Lyly's fondness for extended similes, often drawn from obscure or invented natural lore. Shakespeare pays back-handed homage to Euphuism in *1 Henry IV* when Falstaff and Hal take turns playing the part of a king. Falstaff, we recall, asks for a cup of sack so that he may speak in King Cambyses' vein, but what he speaks is actually in *Euphues'* high-flown vein:

Harry, I do not only marvel where thou spendest thy time, but also how thou art accompanied. For though the camomile, the more it is trodden on, the faster it grows, yet youth, the more it is wasted, the sooner it wears. . . . There is a thing, Harry, which thou hast often heard of, and it is known to many in our land by the name of pitch. This pitch, as ancient writers do report, doth defile. So doth the company thou keepest. For Harry, now I do not speak to thee in drink, but in tears; not in pleasure, but in passion; not in words only, but in woes also. (2. 5. 402–20)

The parody is funny but it falls short of the real thing.

Here, for instance, is part of the explanation of the pseudo-mytho-logical background to Lyly's play *Gallathea* (1588). It was written to be performed by a company of boy actors for an aristocratic audience that included Queen Elizabeth herself. It is worth hearing, not only for the technical skill it exhibits, but also—to use a Euphuistic turn of phrase—for the idea of comedy it embodies:

In times past, where thou seest a heap of small pebble, stood a stately temple of white marble, which was dedicated to the god of the sea (and in right, being so near the sea). . . . But Fortune, constant in nothing but inconstancy, did change her copy, as people their custom. For the land, being oppressed by the Danes who instead of sacrifice committed sacrilege, instead of religion rebellion, and made a prey of that in which they should have made their prayers, tearing down the temple even with the earth, being almost equal with the skies, enraged so the god who binds the winds in the hollows of the earth, that he caused the seas to break their bounds, sith men had broke their vows, and to swell as far above their reach as men had swerved above their reason.[18]

The multiplying symmetries of the language, in which the pattern of sound threatens to take precedence over sense, is apt for romantic comedy; it is an aural equivalent of the plot's insistence on turning a chaos of erotic and political desires into an order of lovers appropri-ately paired within a society newly in accord with itself and its gods.

Like many comic plots, Lyly's language represents a world of infinite complexity contained by an ultimate design of apparently benevolent order.

Shakespeare found more in Lyly than a verbal style. Like *A Midsummer Night's Dream*, the cast of *Gallathea* is drawn from widely differing registers: it is an exercise in finding concord in dramaturgic discord. So one strand of *Gallathea* is concerned with the human problems of its pastoral characters, while another is concerned with the territorial strife between the chaste goddess Diana and the lascivious Venus, while a third interwoven strand involves three lower-class type-characters, Robin, Rafe, and Dick. Lyly is fond of pointing to his (supposed) violations of comic decorum. His prologue to *Midas* uses a kind of sociological analysis to justify the play's failure to observe one kind of unity in order to achieve another kind: 'Traffic and travel hath woven the nature of all nations into ours, and made this land like an arras [tapestry], full of device, which was broadcloth, full of workmanship.' In a mixed up nation, it's only appropriate that plays should also be mixed: 'If we present a mingle-mangle, our fault is to be excused because the whole world is become an hodgepodge."[19] Excusing the fantastic qualities of his play *Endimion*, Lyly claims to be *sui generis*: 'We present neither comedy, nor tragedy, nor story [history], nor anything, but that whosoever heareth may say this, "Why, here is a tale of the Man in the Moon."'[20]

Shakespeare found the matter as well as the manner of Lyly's plays congenial to his own explorations in comedy. Lyly is an Ovidian writer; that is, he takes themes, directly or indirectly, from Ovid's *Metamorphoses*, and he imitates Ovid's blend of romantic passion and coolly ironic detachment. In Lyly as in Ovid, gods and mortals meet and love, or, at least, meet and unchastely chase one another. The defining moment of the Ovidian tale is the moment of metamorphosis, when powerful emotion is both frozen and transformed: the weeping Niobe changed into a fountain, the fleeing Daphne into a tree. In *Gallathea* Lyly plays a teasing variation on Ovidian metamorphosis. A sea monster threatens to destroy the play's pastoral world unless he receives his annual tribute, the most beautiful maiden in the community. Two fathers, each afraid that his daughter will be chosen, disguise the girls, Gallathea and Phyllida, as boys. (Because the best-looking girls aren't available, the frightened mortals try to palm off another girl, Hebe, on the hungry monster—who refuses the offer.) The two girls, wandering in the woods, meet and, each thinking the other is a boy, fall in love; and they remain in love even after they discover the other's true sex. When, in the parallel plot, the battle between the chaste Diana and lusty Venus is resolved, the gods decide to help the girls by transforming one of them into a boy—later, after the play has ended. The moment of transformation is reserved for some indefinite future time, and while the audience knows what it will be, it never learns whose it will be. The heterosexual imperative of the comic marriage-plot is fulfilled without quite dissipating the titillating possibilities of the comedy's same-sex wooing. Shakespeare eagerly followed Lyly's example when he too exploited the permutations and combinations available when a boy actor plays a girl disguised as a boy. We'll look more closely at that Shakespearian situation in the next chapter. Here we can notice that Shakespeare followed Lyly, not only in the matters of costume and kinkiness, but in making love both a madness and the cure for madness, both a disruption of social harmony and the means to renewed harmony, both a matter of individual human silliness and a link between the mortal and divine spheres.

Lyly's comedies were written as homage to the nation's greatest, chastest, most elusive romantic heroine, Queen Elizabeth. And in the works of other playwrights, too, a kind of national comedy took shape in which the elusive female object of masculine desire is, figuratively, England itself. Robert Greene's *Friar Bacon and Friar Bungay* (1590) is, from one point of view, a comic answer to Marlowe's tragedy of the damned magician, Faustus: Friar Bacon renounces the destructive power of his magic, but not until he has used it to aggrandize England. Friar Bacon's is not the only magic at work in Greene's play: Margaret, the fair maid of Fressingfield, is a kind of eroticized personification of England's green and pleasant land, its fertile countryside and game-filled forests; and any man who sees her is enchanted to love her. That love, like Bacon's magic, can be a force for good or ill; along with the promise of fruitful marriage, it brings deadly strife and class-conflict into the play. The critic William Empson brilliantly analyses the effect of Greene's multiple-plot structure:

The process is simply that of dramatising a literary metaphor – 'The power of beauty is like the power of magic'; both are individualistic, dangerous, and outside the social order. But it is so strong that it brings out other ideas which are at the back of the metaphor. It lets Margaret's continual insistence that she is humble and only the keeper's daughter make her into a sort of earth-goddess, and Bacon's magic, though not from Black Magic like Faust's, is from an earth magic he must repent of... The effect on the [friar] is to make [him] 'jolly', connected with low life or the people as a whole.... And it does not seem an irrelevant piece of flattery when Bacon produces a final prophecy in praise of Elizabeth; it was this Renaissance half-worship of Elizabeth and the success of England under her rule that gave conviction to the whole set of ideas.[21]

Friar Bacon and Friar Bungay takes place in a kind of mythical Olde England, and its fun-loving aristocrats and royalty are a far cry from the densely particularized, deeply politicized characters of Shake-speare's history plays. But the comedy's vision of English history as a love story with a happy ending is not irrelevant to Shakespeare's contemporaneous development of 'history' as a genre that alludes to the conventions of both comedy and tragedy. King Harry's wooing of the French princess Catherine at the end of *Henry V* figures the contested land as a woman's sexualized body. 'Is it possible dat I sould love de *ennemi* of France?', asks the conquered Princess; and the King replies,

No, it is not possible you should love the enemy of France, Kate. But in loving me, you should love the friend of France, for I love France so well that I will not part with a village of it, I will have it all mine; and Kate, when France is mine, and I am yours, then yours is France, and you are mine. (5. 2. 169–76)

Her addled response—'I cannot tell vat is dat'—is appropriate, given Harry's mingling of hard-as-nails political realism and Petruccio-like romantic fun-and-games.

The comic idea of Britain as a nubile woman, and of English history as a romantic comedy, was losing some of its charm as the mortal moon, chaste Elizabeth herself, grew closer to death. Some of Shake-speare's contemporaries relocated the comic scene from lush pastoral to urban decay (as Shakespeare does in *Measure for Measure*). And satire—located on Ben Jonson's title-page as an adjunct of tragedy—increasingly infiltrated the space of comedy. Thomas Dekker's *The Shoemaker's Holiday* (1599) is a nostalgic attempt to have things both ways: an urban play in the key of pastoral comedy. The guiding spirit of

Dekker's comedy is Simon Eyre, the jolly shoemaker who rises to become Lord Mayor of London. Eyre's workshop is like an inner-city Forest of Arden where master and servant, aristocracy and middle class can be in accord. The aristocrat Rowland Lacy, who wants to avoid going to war so he can woo his beloved Rose, disguises himself as a Dutch shoemaker and finds work with Simon Eyre. (The other work-men threaten to strike unless Simon hires 'Hans': this at a time when actual London workers were prone to riot against the threat of foreign competition.) Simon helps unite the lovers; in the process he converts the young aristocrat's cash into the commodities which, bought cheap and sold high, make Simon Eyre the richest man in London. Simon's catch-phrase, 'Prince am I none, yet am I princely born', encapsulates the heavy-duty political work of Dekker's comic fantasy, simultan-eously preserving monarchical and aristocratic privilege while seeming to dissolve it in an idea of universal nobility. But by the turn of the century Dekker's optimism is unusual. Increasingly common is a city comedy in which aristocrats and merchants prey upon one another and marriage is the most corrupt of businesses.

The title of Thomas Middleton's biting satire, *A Chaste Maid in Cheapside* (1613), is itself a paradox: in the commercial world of Lon-don's Cheapside, a chaste maid is a fish out of water. In Middleton's play, everything and everyone is for sale; or, more precisely, the dis-tinction between thing and person disappears where both are com-modities. Sir Walter Whorehound comes to London from his Welsh estates to use Mrs Allwit as his personal whore. In Middleton's parody of happy homelife, Sir Walter proudly sires children with Mrs Allwit while Mr Allwit is paid for the pleasure of not having sex with his own wife. That's a single plot-line in one of the most dazzling of all Elizabethan or Jacobean multiple-plot plays. Another line concerns the futile efforts of Sir Oliver and Lady Kix to beget a child who would inherit their kinsman Sir Walter's lands. Since old Kix cannot do it he virtually hires young Touchwood to do it for him. (Touchwood's problem is over-fecundity: like a fertility god gone haywire, he only has to pass through a village to impregnate so many young women that the labour force is diminished and the crops cannot be harvested.) The young man-about-town gets paid to impregnate Lady Kix; Lady Kix gets her pleasure and her children; and the proud non-papa, Sir Oliver, gets Sir Walter Whorehound's forfeited land.

It is a satire on the mutually beneficial relations between land-rich, money-poor country gentry and money-rich, status-poor entrepreneurial citizens. In effect it is also a satire on Shakespearian comedy's marriage-plot—which we'll look at in the next chapter. The comedies of Ben Jonson also tend to be anti-romantic. The wedding in *Epicoene* is between an old man who wants a silent wife and, as he eventually learns, a boy disguised as a girl (not, as in Lyly or Shakespeare, a girl disguised as a boy). In *Volpone* Jonson creates a romantic hero, young Bonario, and a damsel-in-distress, Celia; but they are as separate from one another at the end as at the beginning of Jonson's satire on money-lust and anarchic individualism. The great, sprawling carnival of *Bartholomew Fair* is, in effect, Jonson's comic version of *King Lear*. In his teeming fairground, as on Shakespeare's tragic heath, disguises are stripped away and normative social distinctions are eroded. Jonsonian comedy reminds us of the wide variety of possibilities within the conventions of a single genre. Jonson called Shakespeare's last plays 'mouldy tales', old-fashioned and fantastic. While Jonson in his satires was exposing the seamy underside of contemporary urban life, Shakespeare (whose *Measure for Measure* and *Troilus and Cressida* know all about a world of universal prostitution) was beginning to turn his attention not to satire but to a different arrangement of generic conventions—to his romances, *Pericles*, *Cymbeline*, *The Winter's Tale*, and *The Tempest*, with their magical islands, mysterious mountains, and pastoral retreats, their remorse-ridden fathers and lost children, their torn families in search of wholeness.

In those late plays, as in his earliest, Shakespeare was drawing on received ideas of literary and dramatic form, and wringing fresh surprises from old generic conventions. The following chapters deal more directly with his specific achievements than we've done so far in our introductory look at critical principles and theatrical predecessors. Guided by the order of the genres in the First Folio, we turn in the next chapter to Shakespeare's comedies, and following that—with no better or worse logic than convention itself provides—to his histories and tragedies.

3

Mr William Shakespeare's Comedies

CHRISTOPHER SLY, drunk as a lord, gets to see a play, and that play is the one Shakespeare, who created Sly to be its audience, called *The Taming of the Shrew*. Doctor's orders: 'a pleasant comedy', Sly is told, will cure his melancholy by framing his 'mind to mirth and merriment'. Sly is new to playgoing but he is a critic on instinct (''Tis a very excellent piece of work, madam lady. | Would 'twere done', he comments after scene 1), so his first question is about the play's genre: 'Is not a comonty | A Christmas gambold, or a tumbling trick?' (Induction 2, ll. 133–4). Mispronunciation not withstanding, Sly intuits the historical connection between Elizabethan comedies and recurring festive occasions like May Day, Midsummer Eve, and the last night of Christmas, otherwise known as Twelfth Night. And tumbling tricks is a nice description of comedy's various athleticisms, the fallings down and leapings up of its clowns as well as the verbal gymnastics of its young lovers who pun their way towards the tumbling trick of con-summated sexual desire. But Sly's first attempts at defining 'comonty' are not yet sufficient. Told that comedy is 'more pleasing stuff' than just gambols and tricks, Sly wonders next if it is 'household stuff': nice furniture for a tinker's hovel, maybe, or, more pertinently, the thematic 'stuff' of domesticity, not the great stuff of state affairs but the 'stuff' that leads to marriage, procreation, and family alliances to maintain and extend the Elizabethan household. Like many of Shakespeare's clowns, fools, and drunkards, Sly speaks more wisely than he knows.

Still, Sly's uncertainty about what to expect in a comedy is under-standable. The play he is about to see owes much to older traditions of comedy but it is also an early play in a series of plays most of which had yet to be written at the moment when Sly first enquired about their generic definition. Those plays, Shakespeare's comedies, would change everyone's notion of what a comedy is. Comedy is a genre: it has its traditions, of which Shakespeare was well aware; but the genre is not a mould into which he poured the loose ingredients to be cooked into plays. So after Christopher Sly's attempts to define comedy in terms of its occasion (festival), its means (tricks both physical and verbal), and its content (the creation and continuation of family lines), maybe the Page's non-committal response is an appropriately cautious summary: 'It is', he says, falling back on a word which in Elizabethan usage can signify any narrative regardless of genre, 'a kind of history'.

Things look clearer—perhaps too clear—in retrospect. When Heminges and Condell collected Shakespeare's plays in the Folio of 1623, they listed fourteen comedies. *The Tempest* appears first, *The Winter's Tale* last; there is no discernible reason for the positions of the intervening twelve. In a sense, then, Heminges and Condell were more purely genre critics than their modern successors who supplement classification according to genre with classification according to chronology. These later critics and editors tend to segregate the last-written plays, *The Tempest* and *The Winter's Tale*, along with *Pericles* and *Cymbeline*, in the separate category of 'romances', while the rest, all written between approximately 1588 and 1600, they canonize as *the* comedies and organize in roughly chronological order. (In this chapter I treat the romances for the conventions they share with earlier comedies, and I will return to them when I discuss the tragedies in Chapter 5.) The chronology introduces assumptions about biography—for instance that a writer's first thoughts are less valuable than later thoughts, that young writers are less serious than old, that the older we get the better we are—all of which, however dubious, are difficult to shake off and which, consciously or not, affect judgements about the genre itself.

Modern criticism therefore tends to parcel the comedies, chronologically and formally, into three unequal groups: the 'apprentice' plays, *The Comedy of Errors*, *The Two Gentlemen of Verona*, *Love's Labour's Lost*, and *The Taming of the Shrew*, full of authorial high spirits and the promise of better things to come; the more mature 'festive' or 'golden' comedies, from *A Midsummer Night's Dream* to *Twelfth Night;* and finally the philosophically and formally perplexed 'problem plays', *All's Well that Ends Well*, *Measure for Measure*, and *Troilus and Cressida*, in which the comedian, his attention now turning toward tragedy, has virtually ceased to laugh. There is value in the division: *Measure for Measure's* Vienna is certainly a grimmer setting than *As You Like It's* Forest of Arden, and a comparison of *The Two Gentlemen of Verona* with *Twelfth Night* does suggest that practice makes perfect. But the chronology can be misleading if it suggests a neat development from one play to the next, and it can forestall our answering Sly's implicit questions: Why should these widely various plays be classed as a single kind, and what relationship is there between each individual comedy and the class to which it belongs?

We're all experts in comedy—the meanest thing you can say about a person is that he or she lacks a sense of humour—yet it remains surprisingly difficult for any of us to say what comedy is. We've already noticed the unreliability of the laugh-meter test. The most sharp-witted comic character Shakespeare ever created, Jack Falstaff, comes to life in a play Heminges and Condell classified as history; and with all allowances for historical and cultural difference, it is hard to imagine that Shylock's last exit ever produced howls of laughter. And we've seen that Renaissance theorists had other ways of drawing the line between comedy and tragedy, and that their ways are, for the most part, as unreliable as the laugh-meter test. In the tradition derived from Aristotle, comedy was supposed to deal with characters of middling or low social status, while tragedy deals with characters greater than the norm. Some of Shakespeare's contemporaries observed that distinction, especially in the years after 1600, in satirical city comedies about merchants, their wives, and their business and sexual dealings with members of the lower aristocracy. But Shakespeare's comedies, although they go low enough on the social scale, also rise to include dukes and duchesses, princes and princesses. One implication of the social-class distinction—that what happens to ordinary folks is trivial, hence the stuff of comedy, while what happens to their rulers is the grand work of tragedy—may not be overturned but it is unsettled by the wide social range of Shakespeare's casts of characters.

Scholastic theory applied another test: 'all comedy deals with fictional plots, whereas tragedy is often sought in historical reality.'[1] Here, Shakespearian practice and scholarly theory were roughly in accord. Does it matter? Yes: because the one thing we can say of all historical figures is that, like us, they die; their lives, represented on stage, occur in the shadow of the already finished: they cannot escape the plot of their mortality. The characters of Shakespeare's comedy, on the other hand, are characters of apparently limitless possibility. It is not so much that anything can happen to them as that the one thing necessary in history and tragedy does not happen to them. Shakespeare's comedies know enough about death to avoid it.

Sex, Marriage, and Myths of the Happy Ending

In quest of generic definition we come, then, to the happy ending of comedy versus the unhappy ending of tragedy—a distinction sanctioned by the precedent of ancient theory and by our experience of Shakespeare's plays. We can assert this distinction even knowing that the end of *Measure for Measure* has its problems and that the quality of happiness in *The Merchant of Venice* is decidedly strained. The happiness of Shakespeare's comic endings belongs in some measure to the characters, to that majority of them, at least, who get their heart's desires; and it belongs in some measure to those members of the audience who feel that their hopes for the plot's outcome have been fulfilled. But the happiness of the comic ending belongs also to the plot itself, a simple distinction in what happens: if the main character or characters are dead at the end of the play, it's an unhappy ending and we call that tragedy, but if they're married, it's a happy ending and we call it comedy. The distinction may not correspond to everyone's idea of unhappy versus happy (Hamlet thinks that death is a consummation devoutly to be wished, and Lucio, in *Measure for Measure*, thinks his enforced marriage is 'pressing to death, whipping, and hanging' (5.1.521–2), while Isabella keeps her opinion to herself), but not even the most cynical would claim it is without difference.

There are, of course, exceptions to the comic-marriage rule: the history of any genre is the history of its variations. But the variations are recognizable as such precisely because the pattern is invoked even as it is violated. In *Love's Labour's Lost* Biron objects:

> Our wooing doth not end like an old play.
> Jack hath not Jill. These ladies' courtesy
> Might well have made our sport a comedy.
>   (5. 2. 860–2)

The delay of closure defines what will be necessary, in some always-to-be-anticipated off-stage future, for the comic pattern to be completed. In *The Taming of the Shrew* the wedding day arrives in Act 3, but consummation is delayed: Petruccio on his wedding night makes 'a sermon of continency' (4. 1. 169) to Katherine—it is one of his tactics for making her 'conformable as other household Kates' (2. 1. 272)—so that her consent can be part of the closure. Helen in *All's Well that Ends Well* is, like Kate, married early in the action; but, unlike Kate, it is Helen who contrives the time of consummation and eventually enforces her reluctant husband's consent.

The assertion that a Shakespearian comedy is a play which ends in betrothal, marriage, or the reunion and reconciliation of married couples is in danger of looking less peculiar than it should. At the end of *As You Like It*, a play in which four couples make their way to the altar, Hymen, the god of marriage, pronounces the supposed universality of marriage-as-happy-ending: 'Then is there mirth in heaven, | When earthly things made even | Atone together.... High wedlock then be honourèd' (5. 4. 106–8, 142). By making individuals 'even'—in accord and in pairs—marriage (according to its spokesman) produces divine 'mirth'; heaven's laughter seals this human institution as the means to 'atone' faults which might otherwise cause heaven's sorrow or anger. Hymen's attempt is to universalize and naturalize marriage so that the theatrical and social convention becomes the stamp of a literally divine comedy. But despite his authority, little about the hymeneal imperative of Shakespearian comedy is merely natural—little about it that is not bound to particular cultural circumstances working upon an individual artist's extraordinary sensibility. It was otherwise in the Roman comedies of Plautus, which Shakespeare studied and, in *The Comedy of Errors*, imitated and radically altered. Plautus's *The Menaechmus Twins* ends with one of the twin brothers kicking off the traces of home and leaving a nagging wife behind to be auctioned off to the highest bidder. *The Comedy of Errors*, by contrast, reconciles the wedded couple, finds a wife for the unmarried brother, and after a thirty-three years' separation reunites the twins' father and

mother. And it was otherwise in the comedies of Shakespeare's greatest contemporary in the genre, Ben Jonson. *Volpone* ends with the
characters locked in their individual prisons, literal or metaphorical;
Epicoene ends happily with an annulment; *Bartholomew Fair* turns the
quest for marriage into a predatory game. In light of all this, the
connection between marriage and Shakespeare's comic plotting
requires some explanation.

Marriage licenses sexual desire, where 'license' means both to allow
and to control. The (to us) most private and personal of matters is put
under the aegis of church or state, which exercise power by allowing
individuals to do what, in this case, they want. Jack can have Jill
because the community through its ruling powers permits it. The
role Hymen plays so literally in *As You Like It* is filled in other comedies
by a variety of authority figures. In *A Midsummer Night's Dream*
Theseus exerts his ducal power to tear down the wall of parental
opposition that keeps Hermia and Demetrius apart, granting the
fulfilment of their desire through the assertion of his superior will;
in *The Merchant of Venice* Portia's dead father's 'will' gives its mysterious approval to her choice of Bassanio as husband; in *All's Well that
Ends Well* Helen gets to marry the recalcitrant Bertram because the
King of France empowers her choice; in *The Tempest* Prospero, who
wants Miranda to marry Ferdinand, first puts barriers in their way,
forces Ferdinand to undergo a series of tests, and then presents a
splendid wedding masque to celebrate their betrothal.

As these examples suggest, Shakespeare's comic marriage-plots
accommodate a complex of competing interests; and that accommodation—which dramatically constructs authority as beneficent to
individuals' desires—constitutes part of what we call the happiness of
his comic endings. In each of these comedies, masculine authority,
embodied in duke or father or king, is reaffirmed, but in each of them
the licensing authority has to overrule another, competing, less benevolent masculine authority which would impede rather than facilitate
lovers' desire. Theseus overrules Hermia's father; Portia's dead father
figuratively opposes a living father, Shylock, whose 'bond' is for death
not marriage; the King of France uses his authority to overrule Bertram's narcissistic attachment to his hereditary status which blinds him
to the worth of Helen; Prospero substitutes the tractable Ferdinand for
Caliban, whose desire would take the form of rape rather than mar-

riage. More remarkably, in each of these plays the female characters themselves exercise what, under other conditions, would appear as conventionally masculine authority: Hermia chooses to love whom she will, despite being warned that 'To you your father should be as a god' (*Midsummer Night's Dream*, 1. 1. 47); Portia in masculine disguise wields the authority of lawyer and judge, a 'Daniel come to judgement'; Helen cures the king with medical skills she learned from her father, and as her reward she gets to choose her husband; Miranda chooses Ferdinand despite her father's feigned disapproval. In each case, the comic heroine, whether literally disguised as a man or not, acts on her own behalf but also as the agent of an authority which was frequently, in the world outside comedy, gendered as masculine.

A tumbling trick indeed, this comic feminization of authority, but it is not a trick entirely limited to the fantastic world of comedy. From 1556 to 1603 Queen Elizabeth embodied in her own richly adorned person the paradox—a woman controlling a man's world—which Shakespeare harmonizes, often with difficulty, often incompletely, on his comic stage. Elizabeth governed a nation whose laws tried to make secular fact out of St Paul's injunction that the husband in a Christian marriage should be the head, the lord and master, of his wife. (Elizabeth herself managed the contradiction, on the personal and the political level, by staying single.) Petruccio in *The Taming of the Shrew*, despite the reassuring winks and nudges of his self-parodic super-macho performance, speaks a nearly literal truth about the laws governing Elizabethan marriage when he claims that Kate 'is my goods, my chattels. She is my house, | My household-stuff, my field, my barn, | My horse, my ox, my ass, my anything' (3 .3. 102–4). But it is Kate who holds centre stage in Act 5 to speak the play's longest (and for modern audiences its most controversial) speech; it is Kate who triumphs over the other women and astonishes all the men. Her acceptance of an institution in which 'Thy husband is thy lord, thy life, thy keeper, | Thy head, thy sovereign' (5. 2. 151–2) may be degrading from a modern perspective; equality of the sexes this certainly is not. But on Shakespeare's stage the alliance of Kate and Petruccio signifies comedy's happy ending, and it does so for various related reasons.

Not only is there a kind of personal dramatic power in Kate's position as Petruccio's energetically acquiescent wife. There is social power as well. Elizabethan marriage joined together not only two people but two families; it was a principal means for extending and consolidating a lineage's wealth and influence in the community. *The Taming of the Shrew* is unusually explicit about the financial stakes in Katherine's marriage to Petruccio, but in none of the comedies does Shakespeare gloss over the social and economic conditions which are being negotiated, whether it is a matter of young Fenton, the minor aristocrat, marrying the respectably middle-class Anne Page in *The Merry Wives of Windsor* or the wealthy Portia marrying the impecunious but gentlemanly Bassanio in *The Merchant of Venice*—or Malvolio the steward *not* fulfilling his mad dream of becoming 'Count Malvolio' by marriage to the Countess Olivia in *Twelfth Night*. But Shakespeare's comedies, like his plays in all genres, are never mere transcriptions of the historical conditions which inform them. If Shakespeare's happy endings acknowledge the economic significance of marriage for the larger community, they also, more prominently, celebrate love between individuals—and the happiness resides in the overcoming of potential conflict between the public business of familial alliance and the private business of emotional and sexual compatibility. In *The Taming of the Shrew* Katherine's father, Baptista, clearly states the combination of social and personal, of financial and emotional, factors which are at stake in the marriage: Petruccio accepts Baptista's terms for a dowry and Baptista accepts Petruccio's terms for a settlement if his wife outlives him, but the agreements can only be signed 'when the special thing is well obtained—| That is her love, for that is all in all' (2. 1. 128–9).

Love and money is a potent combination, and Shakespeare's comedies make it all the more potent, to the point of mythic power. The alliance of Kate and Petruccio, like the marriages at the end of many of the comedies, is endowed with a rhetoric of 'wonder', the word which is used repeatedly to describe Kate's apparent transformation. Even in stolid Padua we hear echoes of Hymen's promise that an ending in marriage brings 'joy in heaven': 'Love wrought these miracles' (5. 1. 115), says Lucentio; and Kate's own father thinks 'she is changed as she had never been'—not a 'tamed' version of the old person but a person so entirely new that he adds 'Another dowry', twenty thousand crowns' worth, 'to another daughter' (5. 2. 119–20). Kate's refusal to play the marriageable role apparently played to such perfection by her sister, Bianca, had brought Padua to a state of crisis: there can be no more marrying until the older sister has a husband. Bianca will weep,

Lucentio will pine, the alliances of money and property that Elizabethan marriage makes possible will remain mere dreams, and the
Minola family will remain at odds with itself until Katherine's com-
pliance makes movement possible. The marriage of Kate and Petruccio becomes the socially acceptable equivalent of a fertility ritual; their
indulgence in licensed sexuality brings renewed life to the community.

Shakespeare did not need anthropology to tell him about the
ancient connections between comedy and the rituals and myths which
ensure and explain the cycle of the seasons.[2] The quasi-mythic hero of
Greek Old Comedy wore a gigantic phallus; Petruccio is slightly more
decorous, but his absurdly exaggerated language as he accepts the
challenge of taming Kate—'Have I not in my time heard lions roar?
| Have I not heard the sea, puffed up with winds, | Rage like an angry
boar chafèd with sweat' (1. 2. 199–201)—suggests, however jokingly,
the heroic stakes in his marriage-quest. Christianity revised the
ancient myth of seasonal return in its own celebration of a god's death
and resurrection, and in the process did its best to de-sexualize the
miracle; Shakespeare's comic marriage-plots restore the sexual connection. In Shakespearian comedy the reward of virtue (and sometimes the forgiveness of vice) is the mythically life-giving energy of sex
contained within the licensed arena of marriage.

The connection between comedy and the myth of seasonal return is
clearest in *The Winter's Tale*, which weaves the myth of Proserpine,
also known as Persephone, into its texture. In the ancient myth,
Prosperine, gathering flowers with her mother, Ceres, the goddess of
vegetation, is carried into the underworld by Dis, or Pluto. A deal is
struck: for part of the year Proserpine will live above ground, in the
flowering and fruiting world; for the other, barren months she will stay
below the earth with Dis. In *The Winter's Tale* Leontes' kingdom must
live without an heir, barren, until the lost one, Perdita, is found. She is
repeatedly identified with flowers and flowering, her pastoral world
with the mythic world:

> These your unusual weeds [costume] to each part of you
> Does give a life; no shepherdess, but Flora
> Peering in April's front. This your sheep-shearing
> Is as a meeting of the petty gods,
> And you the queen on't.
>
> (4. 4. 1–5)

Distributing her flowers, Perdita invokes the figure she also embodies: 'O Proserpina, | For the flowers now that, frighted, thou letst fall | From Dis's wagon' (4. 4. 116–18). And in his next play, *The Tempest*, Shakespeare again alludes to the myth of seasonal return. The wedding masque he presents for Ferdinand and Miranda brings Ceres on stage, 'A contract of true love to celebrate' (4. 1. 84). But Ceres will only appear if she is assured that Venus and Cupid (figures of lust rather than of licensed sexuality) are absent: 'Since they did plot | The means that dusky Dis my daughter got', she has forsworn their company.

The marriage-plot, then, is Shakespeare's way of participating in the ancient association of comedy with fertility and futurity; it is his way of rationalizing comedy's triumph over death itself. In *Much Ado About Nothing*, the slandered Hero is 'left for dead'; the jealous Claudio does 'mourning ostentation' over her grave (4. 1. 204, 207); and as 'penance' (5. 1. 265) he agrees to marry, sight unseen, Leonato's supposed niece, 'Almost the copy of my child that's dead' (5. 1. 281). The substitute bride would satisfy the requirements of familial alliance, since (as Leonato explains) his brother's daughter is also his own sole heir. But the marriage restores more than would be contained in a merely social contract. When the new bride unveils herself, Claudio beholds 'Another Hero! ... Hero that is dead!' (5. 4. 62, 65): 'She died, my lord, but whiles her slander lived' (5. 4. 66), Leonato declares; and the Friar promises further explanations to the stunned on-stage audience: 'All this amazement can I qualify | When after that the holy rites are ended | I'll tell you largely of fair Hero's death' (5. 4. 67–9). The full explanation is delayed partly because we, the off-stage audience, do not need to be told the plot of a play we've already seen; we never did think Hero was dead. But partly the explanation is delayed so that the 'amazement' can remain as such, not quite dissipated by explanation or fact. The wonder of the moment—of an apparent death that led through sorrow, contrition, and penance to this representation of renewed life—survives our knowledge that the only real miracle has been Shakespeare's dramatic resuscitation of an old folkloric plot.

In other comedies, too, the delay of promised explanations makes 'wonder seem familiar' (*Much Ado*, 5. 4. 70). *The Comedy of Errors* is one of Shakespeare's earliest experiments in the genre, but in several ways it prefigures work he would do at the end of his career in the romances.

Only in *The Comedy of Errors* and in *The Winter's Tale* does Shakespeare keep the audience as well as the characters ignorant of a crucial plot-detail, so that the ending can be as surprising to us as it is to them. In *The Comedy of Errors* as in *The Winter's Tale* the marriage of young lovers is part of a pattern of joinings and rejoinings in which a family threatened with endless loss is granted a new beginning. In the early play Shakespeare goes far in the direction of slapstick farce, but he also converts that farce—that out-loud laughable banging together of bodies in too tight a space—into an apparent miracle of multiple restorations. When the mistaken identities have been cleared up and the lost have been found, the Abbess, who turns out to be the mother of the twins and wife of their death-doomed father, promises a full accounting of 'this sympathizèd one day's error' (5. 1. 400)—later, when they will 'hear at large discoursèd all our fortunes' (5. 1. 398). But her language immediately restores the wonder which the post-production narrative will supposedly dispel: 'Thirty-three years have I but gone in travail | Of you, my sons, and till this present hour | My heavy burden ne'er deliverèd' (5. 1. 403–5). The loss was merely labour leading to this birth: 'After so long grief, such nativity!' (5. 1. 409).[3]

And in *The Winter's Tale* Shakespeare's characters do not state but literally stage the idea that death is a passing episode within the comic plot of restoration. Hermione is memorialized in a statue, and the statue comes to life. Shakespeare does not expect us to 'believe' that a real Hermione was really dead and has now really been reborn: that would not only be blasphemous; it would violate the condition of theatrical fiction. We do not literally 'believe' anything that happens on stage; and yet, in the special way art allows, we know that within the fiction all that happens is true. When Paulina leads Leontes into the chapel where she keeps the statue of Hermione, she requires that 'You do awake your faith' (5. 3. 95). The stone turns to flesh and strikes 'all that look upon with marvel'. Shakespeare gives the faithless a way out: we can say that Hermione wasn't really dead, only hiding for sixteen years. But by the same token, Hermione, Leontes, Perdita, and the rest were never really alive, except in the special way that any art is alive, whether inscribed in stone or on the bodies of actors and actresses. 'If this be magic, let it be an art | Lawful as eating' (5. 3. 110–11), says Leontes. As lawful—and as fantastic—as the art of Shakespearian comedy.

The rhetoric of wonder is frequent in the comedies. It does not always rise to the sublime level of the late romances—of, for instance, *Pericles*, where the grieving father's reunion with his storm-torn daughter is accompanied, to his ears, with the music of the spheres. In *The Two Gentlemen of Verona* Proteus does just about everything he can, including attempted rape, to make himself a villain. But his friend Valentine forgives him for his assault against Sylvia, as does Proteus's spurned lover, Julia. Proteus is instantly ashamed of his 'inconstancy' and rewarded with marriage to Julia. A further flurry of forgivenesses quickly follows; and the end, as we might now expect, is the starting over of the dramatic narrative: 'Come, Proteus', says Valentine, ''tis your penance but to hear | The story of your loves discoverèd. | That done, our day of marriage shall be yours, | One feast, one house, one mutual happiness.' (5. 4. 168–71). The explanation for this confluence of happinesses will be the retelling, off-stage, of the plot of *The Two Gentlemen of Verona*. That plot will never be a favourite, even among Shakespeare's greatest fans, but it is at least explicable as one in a series of restless experiments with comedy's capacity to rescue its characters from the potential disaster of their own humanity.

In this early play, Proteus's 'penance' may seem all too easy; in later plays the mysteries are deeper, the explanations more difficult, and the narrative attempt to rationalize more desperate. The end of *All's Well that Ends Well* is literally a riddle about life and death: 'Dead though she be she feels her young one kick. | So there's my riddle; one that's dead is quick' (5. 3. 304–5). Bertram will take his part in the happy ending only if the riddle can be answered—and his paternity proved: 'If she, my liege, can make me know this clearly | I'll love her dearly, ever ever dearly' (5. 3. 317–18). The King too demands a narrative clarification: 'Let us from point to point this story know | To make the even truth in pleasure flow' (5. 3. 326–7). But the truth-telling will wait, and not only for the technical reason that the audience already knows what the characters must learn. In the anxiously problematized world of this late comedy, 'knowing' may pose a threat rather than offer a confirmation of seeming miracles. 'All yet *seems* well', the king says, but his grammar is troubled by a conditional clause: 'and if it end so meet, | The bitter past, more welcome is the sweet' (5. 3. 334–5). In *All's Well*, as in his next comedy, *Measure for Measure*, Shakespeare challenges the happy ending's formal and rhetorical claims by invoking our knowledge that in other genres death is ending, not new beginning, and that sometimes marriages fail. And all the comedies acknowledge, more or less explicitly, the fragility of their own generic claims; they acknowledge that comedy is not the hermetically sealed opposite of tragedy. In *The Winter's Tale*, when Perdita wishes she had the appropriate flowers for Florizel, 'To strew him o'er and o'er', Florizel's shocked response is, 'What, like a corpse?' (4. 4. 129). Where life is most intense its fleetingness may also be most apparent: Perdita's flowers evoke the death they are meant to banish. The rhetoric of comic wonder knows it can be challenged; rather than exclude our sceptical awareness, Shakespeare acknowledges it as one of comedy's potentials.

Comic Identity: Character, Language, Gender

Between the perhaps too-easy accommodation in *Two Gentlemen* and the resistance in *All's Well* is the balance of *Twelfth Night*. In the antagonism between Feste (whose name means festivity) and Malvolio (ill will) *Twelfth Night* stages the contest between comic licence and its sceptical opposition. In his own right Feste can stand as an emblem for Shakespearian comedy's ambivalent self-awareness; he is an edgy, even a disturbing comic presence, a licensed but, as Malvolio reminds him, not a tenured fool. Orsino tries to tip Feste for his singing:

> ORSINO There's for thy pains.
> FESTE No pains, sir. I take pleasure in singing, sir.
> ORSINO I'll pay thy pleasure then.
> FESTE Truly, sir, and pleasure will be paid, one time or
> another.
>
> (2. 4. 66–70)

The price that pleasure exacts is the burden of the Fool's song at the end of the play: with each cheekily dismissive 'hey, ho', he responds with the sound of 'the wind and the rain'; the last verse balances comedy's long view ('A great while ago the world begun') against tragic brevity ('that's all one, our play is done'); and the idea of 'play' immediately acknowledges a more daily grind: 'we'll strive to please you every day'.

As I continue the exploration of Shakespearian comedy, I will occasionally pause over *Twelfth Night* as a kind of moving focus for observing the genre's conventions, expectations, and new departures. In what follows I look at the idea of comic character, comedy's relation to ideas of identity, and the kinds of recognition comedy stages; at the gender issues raised not only in the comic plot (including the plot of a woman disguised as a man), but also in the comic language of word-play and witty dialogue; and at the tensions of a genre that is both expansive and exclusive, the antagonist and the ally of social order.

The title names an occasion: Twelfth Night is the end of the Christmas season. It was, in C. L. Barber's term, a 'festive' time,[4] full of the stuff named in Orsino's first line: music, food, play, and excess in all of them. But as the last night of the Christmas season it could be a desperate time as well, a night-time of indulgence before the inevitable morning-after—and Orsino's line captures that sense of too-muchness as well. Again, in full:

> If music be the food of love, play on,
> Give me excess of it that, surfeiting,
> The appetite may sicken and so die.

Twelfth Night, like Twelfth Night, has its carnival elements, not only the subverting of Malvolio's authority over the aristocratic household's 'place, persons, [and] time' (2. 3. 88) but also Viola's disguise as the ambiguously masculine 'Cesario'—her challenge, that is, to the fixed gender-roles which are society's most visible markers of daytime authority. But this Twelfth Night's revels have a dangerous edge to them. Malvolio is not the only character to feel the threat of madness. Antonio, Sebastian, Olivia, even Viola: each, as they become caught up in their comedy of errors, feels a threat to the supposedly fixed boundaries of personal identity.

The Twelfth Night holiday is also a holy day otherwise known as the Feast of Epiphany. The Greek word means manifestation, showing forth—as in the 'recognition scene' that technically ends a play, when identities are revealed. Shakespeare's *Twelfth Night* may have had its first performance at an actual Twelfth Night celebration in an aristocratic household; more importantly, the play imitates the nature of the holiday/holy day from which it takes its title: it is a play of epiphanies or recognitions, mingling festivity with wonder at mysteries discovered.

What is under wraps and awaiting discovery? What is recognized in the last acts of Shakespearian comedy? We can call it 'identity'—this person named Cesario is actually Viola, and that person you thought was Cesario is actually Sebastian, and the person who loves her is Orsino, who thought he loved Olivia until it was discovered that Olivia is the person who loves Sebastian, who she thought was Cesario—but first we need to submit the idea of identity to the special circumstances of Elizabethan comedy. And we can recall that, relative to the distinctly individualized characters of tragedy, there is an oddly modular quality to the characters of comedy. Desdemona and Othello, Ophelia and Hamlet, Cordelia and Lear: no one has trouble remembering who should go with whom. But Viola, Olivia, Orsino, Cesario, and even Malvolio threaten, as least in their names, to be anagrams of one another.

With *A Midsummer Night's Dream* readers (if not audiences) can sometimes forget whether Hermia or Helena goes with Lysander or Demetrius—and why not, since the characters themselves sometimes forget? One woman is tall and one is short; to themselves they seem, most of the time, absolutely distinct, unique. But Helena reminds Hermia of a deeper connectedness: 'we grew together, | Like to a double cherry: seeming parted, | But yet an union in partition, | Two lovely berries moulded on one stem' (3. 2. 209–12.) In the dark woods, far from the daylight distinctness of Athens, that sublime connectedness becomes a joke about indistinction: Lysander-Hermia-Demetrius-Helena are in Puck's eyes merely the generic Jacks-and-Jills. Comedy's cavalier treatment of human difference can be a blow to the pride of individuals in the western cultural tradition; we like to think of ourselves as unique, irreplaceable. Bertram or Angelo can be tricked into accepting the appropriate mate because one warm body in bed is supposed to feel pretty much like another warm body; the 'bed trick' and other feats of substitution—in *Measure for Measure*, for instance, of one dead prisoner's head for another dead prisoner's head—can only be performed by and on characters whose identities are less distinctly differentiated than, we like to think, our own. The insult to character is, however, balanced by gain. We can laugh when Antipholus of Syracuse, who looks exactly like Antipholus of Ephesus, smacks Dromio of Ephesus because he looks exactly like Dromio of Syracuse (or the other way round) because in comedy, where everyone is the same, no one (almost) gets hurt, much. The modularity of comic characters also permits the duplication of comic characters, so that, in principle, every odd character can find another odd character to make an even pair.

Identity in comedy and identity in tragedy, then, are matters of perspective. From where Puck sits, all Athenians look alike; as a class, 'What fools these mortals be'. Puck sees systems, not individuals. Biron, in *Love's Labour's Lost*, confesses that he is in love, then climbs a tree to watch as first one companion, then another, and then another enters and confesses that he too is in love: 'Like a demigod here sit I in the sky, | And wretched fools' secrets heedfully o'er-eye' (4. 3. 76–7). From Biron's Puckish position, the successive lovers are just 'More sacks to the mill'. Closer to the ground things look different. In *A Midsummer Night's Dream*, when Hermia wakes from her dream of sexual betrayal into its reality, her terror is palpable: alone, in the middle of the dark woods, 'Either death or you I'll find immediately'. The actress (or, in Shakespeare's time, the actor) playing Hermia must realize that terror, and in order to do so must inhabit Hermia's position—must become, that is, blind to what the audience, from its demigod-like position, knows: that what Puck screwed up he can as easily unscrew. Mistaken identity is rife in Shakespeare's early comedies but it is not just a gimmick Shakespeare used when he was a beginner. In *Cymbeline*, Innogen mistakes the headless corpse of the villain Cloten for that of her husband, Posthumus. She is not alone in mistaking identities: her brothers cannot penetrate her disguise as a boy even after her supposed death. Only in the fifth act's notorious cascade of recognitions are identities revealed, as husband and wife, father and daughter and sons recover themselves in the recovery of their relationships.

In the comedies, then, the 'identity' that is discovered in the unfolded plot is not a buried kernel of previously suppressed selfhood. It is an identity that exists by virtue of relationships with other characters whose identities are also grounded in the relationship, so that comic characters may be said to have discovered themselves when they have discovered the child or parent, brother or sister, the friend or lover or husband or wife whose reciprocal identity defines their own. To find oneself in Shakespeare's comedies is to find the other, and to be found is to be not a self alone.

Each of the comedies experiments differently with the ratios between characters' distinctiveness and the ease with which they can be manipulated into, out of, and back into relationships. In *The Merry Wives of Windsor* Falstaff thinks he can substitute for the husbands in their marital beds, while the jealous husband, Ford, believes that Falstaff has actually succeeded. But the wives, Mrs Ford and Mrs Page, never forget who's who; they can play upon their husbands' suspicions and Falstaff's absurd self-love, and at the appropriate time expose each for what he really is. In *Measure for Measure* the Duke tries to stand outside the action, like a Puck with gravitas, manipulating a cast of puppets; but the plot spins out of his control, and what might, as a technical matter of plotting, have been a comedy of errors runs up against the perverse and very human unwillingness of the characters to play their conventional roles. *Troilus and Cressida* is, as usual, an exception which proves the rule. Cressida takes Diomedes as a substitute for Troilus; but Troilus, unwilling to believe that, from Cressida's point of view, one male protector is as good as another, thinks that her action calls into question 'the rule in unity itself', the very principle of individuation: where there should be one Cressida, now there are two—his Cressida and Diomedes' Cressida, each identical to the other, like comic twins who have strayed into a tragic landscape.

Viola's position in *Twelfth Night* is somewhere between that of an all-seeing Puck and a stumbling Hermia: she knows the cause of confusion but she doesn't know how to end it. Viola's summary of the action is supposedly meant to clarify matters but her twisting rhetoric only tangles them further:

> How will this fadge? My master loves her dearly,
> And I, poor monster, fond as much on him,
> And she, mistaken, seems to dote on me.
> What will become of this? As I am man,
> My state is desperate for my master's love.
> As I am woman, now, alas the day,
> What thriftless sighs shall poor Olivia breathe!
> O time, thou must untangle this, not I.
> It is too hard a knot for me t'untie.
>
> (2. 2. 33–41)

Viola knows this much, which is more than any other character knows, but no more. The audience, however, knows the rest.

We know it, not exactly from the start but, rather, from scene 2. The first scene presents the stand-off between the mooning Orsino and the mourning Olivia. By the scene's end, Shakespeare has established all that might be needed for the plot of a good-enough comedy: he has given the audience the expectation of a pairing between these two desperately eligible people, and, in Olivia's refusal, an impediment. How will these two isolated characters discover the relationships which will produce their Twelfth Night's recognition? Enter, in scene 2, Viola, fresh from the sea.

Here is a possible solution and a new complication. And here too is a type of comic character which Shakespeare did not invent but did remake with stunning effect and historical consequence. Even Christopher Sly wouldn't be surprised at the way Viola deals with the fact that she is shipwrecked in a country ruled by an eligible bachelor: 'conceal me what I am, and be my aid | For such disguise as haply shall become | The form of my intent' (1. 2. 49–51). The young woman who disguises herself as a boy was a staple of the non-dramatic tales, or romances, from which Shakespeare drew some of his plots, both comic and tragic; and we've seen that she had previously appeared on stage in Lyly's *Gallathea*, where boy-actors played the part of girls-disguised-as-boys. Shakespeare himself began exploiting the comic potential of the girl-disguised-as-boy with Julia in *The Two Gentlemen of Verona*, hit his stride with Portia in *The Merchant of Venice*, Rosalind in *As You Like It*, and Viola in *Twelfth Night*, and was still at it near the end of his career, with Innogen in *Cymbeline*. Critics have tried to specify the figure's appeal to contemporary audiences and, what amounts to the same thing, its horror for contemporary opponents of the stage: did they see on stage the body of a boy or of a girl or of a feminized boy? Did they see the boy being wooed by another boy, or the girl being wooed by another girl, or did they keep it straight and see the girl and the boy wooing each other? The right answer is surely all-of-the-above, but it is an answer that raises related questions for comedy as a genre.

With the problematic exceptions of Juliet, Cleopatra, and, possibly, Lady Macbeth, there are, in Shakespeare's plays, no tragic heroines. Women suffer in the tragedies, but the very titles, which are men's names, tell us that tragedy, in comparison to comedy, is a man's world. It would be too optimistic simply to reverse the ratio and claim that comedy is a woman's world. The heroines of Shakespeare's comic marriage-plots perform wonders on their own behalf but they also help to make their world safe for men's cultural privilege. In *The Merchant of Venice* Portia presides over the trial of the caskets and gets Bassanio as her prize, to whom immediately she commits 'her gentle spirit . . . to be directed | As from her lord, her governor, her king. | Myself and what is mine to you and yours | Is now converted' (3. 2. 163–7). But the girl-disguised-as-a-boy also changes what she preserves: after Rosalind, in *As You Like It*, has made Orlando jump through hoops to woo the androgynous figure called Ganymede, the distribution of gendered power, on stage and possibly even in the society staged, will never look quite the same.

The social androgyny of Shakespeare's comic heroines (whether literally disguised or not) derives not only from their physical embodiment by boy-actors; it derives also from the doubleness of their embodiment in language. All dramatic characters are made out of words, but these comic heroines assume a conventionally masculine power to control the language of their self-creation. In the tragedies men get the soliloquies: Hamlet may or may not be mad but he sure does talk, while Ophelia is silenced until she really is mad ('You need not tell us what Lord Hamlet said; | We heard it all', says Polonius after he has 'loosed' his daughter to the Prince (3. 1. 182–3)). But in the comedies the big speeches are as likely to belong to a Portia as to a Shylock; and regardless of size, they are speeches of power which undo masculine folly or rage, and permit comic closure. Portia, disguised as Balthazar, becomes not just a temporary lawyer but a lord of language, wresting the words of the law from Shylock and finding in its lexicon the 'mercy' which even the Duke could not constrain.

Like Portia, Rosalind, in *As You Like It*, takes control of the play's language and manipulates its central symbols. Orlando writes his bad love poems and publishes them on Arden's trees, but Rosalind gets to interpret and correct them. His sweetly fatuous effort to allegorize her as a Helen or Cleopatra, Atalanta or Lucretia (3. 2. 142–5) is countered by her sharper criticism: 'O most gentle Jupiter! What tedious homily of love have you wearied your parishioners withal' (3. 2. 152–3). Orlando tells Rosalind, disguised as Ganymede, that he will die if Rosalind will not have him; Rosalind's response rewrites a whole library of myths about heroically suffering male lovers:

The poor world is almost six thousand years old, and in all this time there was not any man died in his own person, videlicet, in a love-cause. Troilus had his brains dashed out with a Grecian club, yet he did what he could to die before, and he is one of the patterns of love. Leander, he would have lived many a fair year though Hero had turned nun if it had not been for a hot midsummer night, for, good youth, he went but forth to wash him in the Hellespont and, being taken with the cramp, was drowned; and the foolish chroniclers of that age found it was Hero of Sestos. But these are all lies. Men have died from time to time, and worms have eaten them, but not for love. (4. 1. 88–101)

Rosalind-as-Ganymede does not only debunk the old myths of romantic love, with their suffering men and heartless women. 'In [her] own person' she writes a powerful new version of romantic love, in which a woman is the agent of her own desires. Ganymede's doublet-and-hose makes the figure on stage available to a range of erotic fantasies, but in the plot of her own comedy Rosalind-as-Ganymede calls the shots: 'Come, woo me, woo me, for now I am in a holiday humour, and like enough to consent' (4. 1. 64–5). She dictates the script to Orlando: 'you must say, "I take thee, Rosalind, for wife"', and Orlando does as he is told.

   In the later 'problem' comedies the contest for control of the play's language is more difficult and the outcome more ambiguous. In *All's Well that Ends Well* Helen's rival for Bertram's affection is his false friend, Paroles, 'a notorious liar [and] a great way fool' (1. 1. 99–100), whose very name (from the French *parole*) designates him a man of words. Paroles is 'crushed with a plot' (4. 3. 326), but it is not of Helen's making. He sets himself up with his boasting (like Falstaff in *1 Henry IV*) and his fellow soldiers bring him down with a barrage of nonsensical sounds. For her part, Helen wins Bertram's body by substituting her own body in bed for Diana's, but the end of the play gives no great assurance that she has won his mind. And in *Measure for Measure* Isabella tries desperately *not* to be the heroine of a romantic comedy, not to write for herself a plot like Rosalind's or Viola's. When we first see her she is eager to enter a nunnery where 'you must not speak with men | But in the presence of the prioress. | Then if you speak, you must not show your face; | Or if you show your face, you must not speak' (1. 4. 10–13). She wants to escape the world of sex and procreation figured in all its ugly as well as attractive vitality by Vienna's brothels, johns, pimps, and whores. But the world rudely intrudes in the person of

Lucio, bringing news that her brother is condemned to die because 'He hath got his friend with child' (1. 4. 29). To save Claudio's life Isabella must use the power she has to 'move men' (1. 2. 172); she must become, despite herself, a witty worker in words like Rosalind or Portia, Kate, Beatrice, or Viola. And in her great series of one-to-one debates, first with Angelo, then with Claudio, Isabella proves her right to membership in that company.

In those tense scenes we hear language being used as an intellectual weapon, and at the same time we hear language using its speaker, producing effects she does not intend and cannot control, 'breeding' a 'sense' in Angelo which is exactly the opposite of the sense she thinks she means. Isabella speaks the arguments of restraint, self-control, chastity to this 'man of stricture and firm abstinence' (1. 3. 12); but as Angelo takes up each argument, and she responds, and as they match each other in strength and in weakness, the debate comes to seem more like a dance, and the music, angry and discordant though it is, is the food of erotic engorgement. Distantly we recognize in Isabella a version of the veiled Olivia, in Angelo the narcissistic Orsino. In the blighted cityscape of Vienna we recognize a meaner version of the woods outside of Athens, and in the Duke a more seriously intentioned and a more seriously blundering version of Puck. As in a nightmare version of the Athenian lovers' dream, bodies and bodyparts are easily transferable, a maidenhead for a maidenhead, a head for a head, a head for a maidenhead. But for all those punning substitutions, and for all the characters' verbal agility, at the end of Act 5 Isabella is silent; there are no words in her script to reply to the Duke's proposal of marriage.

The quibble, or pun, said Samuel Johnson in the eighteenth century, was Shakespeare's 'fatal Cleopatra'; he was 'content to lose the world' for the sake of a good, or even a bad, play on words.[5] *Measure for Measure* shows that Shakespeare knew how dangerous it can be to play with words. Elsewhere in the comedies, however, he shows how much fun it can be. Punning is not necessarily a woman's game and is certainly not confined to comedy, but it is a game that can be played as well by conventionally marginal characters as by their supposed social betters. Clowns and fools, like Feste, are champions of wordplay; and when a fool plays with a girl-disguised-as-a-boy, the results can be dazzling:

> VIOLA Dost thou live by thy tabor?
>
> FESTE No, sir, I live by the church.
>
> VIOLA Art thou a churchman?
>
> FESTE No such matter, sir. I do live by the church for I do
> live at my house, and my house doth stand by the
> church.
>
> VIOLA So thou mayst say the king lies by a beggar if a
> beggar dwells near him, or the church stands by thy
> tabor if thy tabor stand by the church.
>
> FESTE You have said, sir. To see this age!—A sentence is
> but a cheverel glove to a good wit, how quickly the
> wrong side may be turned outward.
>
> VIOLA Nay, that's certain. They that dally nicely with
> words may quickly make them wanton.
>
> (3. 1. 1–15)

And so on: between them Viola and Feste have turned a musical instrument (his tabor) into a sexy woman (a 'wanton')—a comic rather than a fatal Cleopatra. Where Dr Johnson wanted language to define and clarify, to make things single, comedy complicates and splits, finds doubles (the church stands by the tabor as well as the tabor by the church); it makes language fertile, and the births are multiple. A pun pushes more meanings into a word than the word can hold, and the result is that little explosion which the hearer acknowledges with an 'ooph' of recognition. The pun is at the level of rhetoric what farce is at the level of plot: too much likeness in too small a space. It splits apart meanings and brings them together in new combinations. It is contemptuous of hierarchy, boundaries, and decorum. It finds sex everywhere.

When agile characters volley words in 'a set of wit well played' (*Love's Labour's Lost*, 5. 2. 29) the meanings can spin too fast for any audience to take them all in. But we can still judge the progress of the game. We can hear aggression being eroticized and see competitiveness become admiration. (The scenes between Isabella and Angelo in *Measure for Measure* are a grim variant of that progress.) In *Love's Labour's Lost* it is not a woman but four young men who try to 'war against [their] own affections | And the huge army of the world's desires' (1. 1. 9–10). They create an all-male academy and dedicate themselves to improving their minds. Enter four young ladies: the

men and women joust, matching rhyme to rhyme, twisting one
another's metaphors, completing one another's lines:

> BIRON Your wit's too hot, it speeds too fast, 'twill tire.
> ROSALINE Not till it leave the rider in the mire.
> BIRON What time o' day?
> ROSALINE The hour that fools should ask.
> BIRON Now fair befall your mask.
> ROSALINE Fair fall the face it covers.
> BIRON And send you many lovers.
> ROSALINE Amen, so you be none.
> BIRON Nay, then I will be gone.
>
> (2. 1. 119–27)

Here Rosaline wins a point from 'Biron, the merry madcap lord'.
('Not a word with him but a jest', 'And every jest but a word', 'It
was well done of you to take him at his word', 'I was as willing
to grapple as he was to board' (2. 1. 215–18)—and off it spins again.)
Win, lose, or draw, we know there will have to be a rematch. But
the end of the play, when the men hope that they have manœuvred
the women towards marriage, is only a rain-delay: the men will have
to purge themselves of linguistic excess before 'these ladies'
courtesy [makes] our sport a comedy' (5. 2. 861–2). In *Love's Labour's
Lost* (to finish these bad athletic metaphors) the men's wit scores an
own-goal.

In *Love's Labour's Lost* the women control the ending, or lack of it.
The balance of power is less clear at the end of *The Taming of the Shrew*,
a play in which woman's speech is a central dramatic issue. Petruccio
makes his first move by trying to take possession of a name:

> Good morrow, Kate, for that's your name I hear.
> KATHERINE Well have you heard, but something hard of
> hearing.
> They call me Katherine that do talk of me.
> PETRUCCIO You lie, in faith, for you are called plain Kate,
> And bonny Kate, and sometimes Kate the curst,
> But Kate, the prettiest Kate in Christendom,
> Kate of Kate Hall, my super-dainty Kate—
> For dainties are all cates, and therefore 'Kate'—
>
> (2. 1. 182–9)

A 'Katherine' is a person in control of herself, a 'Kate' is a sweet snack ('cate'); and at the end of Act 5 it will sound to many listeners as though Petruccio has swallowed it whole: 'Come on, and kiss me, Kate. . . . Come, Kate, we'll to bed' (5. 2. 185, 189). Whether Katherine/Kate has won a husband or lost an identity is less a question of textual fact than of differing production choices and shifting historical values. We can disagree about whether she is at her best standing up to Petruccio or lying down with him. Either way, actresses agree that it's a part to die for: her character is interesting precisely because of the pressure she puts on the expected curves of comic action, resisting where a more conventional heroine would comply, complying where another would resist.

The verbal violence of the word-games in *The Taming of the Shrew* comes close at times to physical violence, as it does also in *The Comedy of Errors*. This is language as slapstick. It's the kind of thing that gives comedy a bad name, and keeps the audience coming. Dromio of Ephesus finds the doors of his house locked against him by the usurping Dromio of Syracuse. He calls to his fellow servants: 'Maud, Bridget, Marian, Cicely, Gillian, Ginn!' and is answered:

> Mome, malt-horse, capon, coxcomb, idiot, patch!
> Either get thee from the door or sit down at the hatch.
> Dost thou conjure for wenches, that thou call'st for
>   such store
> When one is too many? Go, get thee from the door.
> DROMIO OF EPHESUS What patch is made our porter? My
>   master stays in the street.
> DROMIO OF SYRACUSE Let him walk from whence he
>   came, lest he catch cold on's feet.

> (3. 1. 31–7)

The jingling rhymes, the four-stress metre, and the sheer lack of good taste are Shakespeare's homage to the earlier interludes, for instance *Gammer Gurton's Needle*:

> HODGE Tom Tankard's cow (by Gog's bones) she set me
>   up her sail,
>   And flinging about his half acre, fisking with her tail,
>   As though there had been in her arse a swarm of bees,
>   And had not cried, 'Tphrowh, whore!' she'd leaped out
>   of his leas.

DICCON Why, Hodge, lies the cunning in Tom Tankard's
cow's tail?
HODGE Well, I have heard some say that such tokens do
not fail.[6]

But in *The Comedy of Errors* this style of slapstick and farce plays off
against an alternative style of wonder and romance. Both in its own
right and as counterpoint, the Dromios' tumbling, unconstrainable
language echoes the comedy's concern with lost identity, fractured
selfhood, and the desire for a complementary Other who could
make the characters whole:

ANTIPHOLUS OF EPHESUS What art thou that keep'st me
out from the house I owe?
DROMIO OF SYRACUSE The porter for this time, sir, and
my name is Dromio.
DROMIO OF EPHESUS O villain, thou hast stol'n both
mine office and my name.

(3. 1. 42–4)

Already, that is, in *The Comedy of Errors*, as in *The Taming of the Shrew*,
Shakespeare has attached this free-floating, high-spirited, insult-
laden comic language to character. In the matches between Kate and
Petruccio or Rosaline and Biron he has eroticized that comic language.
He has brought the slapstick verse of the interludes into contact with
the sublimer symmetries of John Lyly's prose to create a style in which
characters can wise-crack their way from antagonism to love. The
'merry war' between Beatrice and Benedick in *Much Ado About Nothing*—'They never meet but there's a skirmish of wit between them' (1. 1.
60–1)—is the apotheosis of that style. It takes a satiric energy as
ancient as Aristophanes' Old Comedy and puts it in the service of
the New Comedy of romance. What it gives to the future of the genre
is as important as what it takes from the past. Shakespeare's example
makes possible all the bickering odd-couples of stage and screen, from
Congreve's Mirabell and Millamant to the various Hollywood incar-
nations, from Spencer Tracy and Katherine Hepburn to Billy Crystal's
Harry meeting Meg Ryan's Sally.

Beatrice and Benedick need a little help from their friends to convert
passionate celibacy into a determination that 'The world must be

peopled' (2. 3. 229). In *Twelfth Night* the character who needs to be person-handled into love is Olivia, and the handler (since Olivia refuses to talk to Orsino) is Viola. Olivia is in mourning, but she has other reasons too for resisting Duke Orsino's importunity. She is a countess, which is a great thing to be in Illyria but not so great as a duke; and she will not, we are told, marry above herself. She will not, that is, give up control of her own aristocratic household by dwindling into a wife even if in the process she is enlarged to a duchess. She has servants, retainers, and sponging relatives: all the stuff of aristocratic power. To retain her power intact she resists, in effect, the compromise between empowerment and collaboration with male authority that is inherent in the marriageable heroine's role. Resisting Orsino's stereo-typically masculine fawning and bullying is a cinch. But there is no resisting the sexually and socially ambiguous power of Viola-dis-guised-as-Cesario.

Orsino sends 'Cesario' to woo on his behalf because 'Cesario' looks so fetchingly like a girl:

> Diana's lip
> Is not more smooth and rubious; thy small pipe
> Is as the maiden's organ, shrill and sound,
> And all is semblative a woman's part.
>
> (1. 4. 31–4)

And that, though it takes four more acts for him to find it out, will solve Orsino's problem. Olivia's problem begins when she allows herself to banter provocatively with this 'boy':

> OLIVIA Where lies your text?
> VIOLA In Orsino's bosom.
> OLIVIA In his bosom? In what chapter of his bosom?
> VIOLA To answer by the method, in the first of his heart.
> OLIVIA O, I have read it. It is heresy. Have you no more to say?
> VIOLA Good madam, let me see your face.
> OLIVIA Have you any commission from your lord to negotiate with my face? You are now out of your text. But we will draw the curtain and show you the picture.
>
> (1. 5. 214–23)

Olivia unveils; she participates with face and body, now, as well as words in the aggressive play which, in Shakespearian comedy, can (but doesn't always) become erotic love.

The sexual possibilities and dangers are complicated enough when, all at once, a woman (Olivia) woos a woman (Viola), and a social superior (Olivia) woos a social inferior (Cesario), and a boy actor playing a woman woos a boy actor playing a woman playing a boy. The possibilities are even more complicated, but also more easily containable within the marriage-plot's symmetry of gender-difference, when one of those figures has an identical twin of the opposite sex. The cross-wooing, like a pun, is a situation of comic too-much-ness. All Sebastian has to do is appear on stage at the same time as Viola for the pressure to explode—at last!—in laughter. But the recognition scene in *Twelfth Night* is in fact an oddly muted affair, not exactly unfunny but mixed with other possible responses. Sebastian and Viola seem to grope their way, not only from opposite sides of the stage but from opposite ends of the earth, to mutual recognition. They discover each other step by almost absurd step in a long moment that balances between wonder and a parody of all such scenes of wonder in romances from ancient Greece to Elizabethan England:

> SEBASTIAN Do I stand there? I never had a brother,
>   Nor can there be that deity in my nature
>   Of here and everywhere. I had a sister,
>   Whom the blind waves and surges have devoured.
>   Of charity, what kin are you to me?
>   What countryman? What name? What parentage?
>
> (5. 1. 224–30)

Instead of rushing into each other's arms, Viola and Sebastian lingeringly explore the conventional signs of recognition. Not only do they look exactly alike, not only did their fathers have the same name and die on the same day, but: 'My father had a mole upon his brow.' 'And so had mine!'

This is the kind of thing Gilbert and Sullivan had a ball with, three hundred years later, in their comic operas of lost siblings and infants switched at birth. In the Victorian farce *Box and Cox* the long-lost brothers recognize each other through the absence of any distinguishing bodily mark:

BOX You'll excuse the apparent insanity of the remark,
   but the more I gaze on your features, the more I'm
   convinced that you're my long-lost brother.
COX The very observation I was going to make to you!
BOX Ah—tell me—in mercy tell me—have you such a
   thing as a strawberry mark on your left arm?
COX No!
BOX Then it is he! (*They rush into each other's arms*).[7]

Oscar Wilde, in the greatest English comedy after Shakespeare's
comedies, ends *The Importance of Being Earnest* with a parodic homage
to the genre conventions of *Twelfth Night*. What is discovered is
merely a name, the empty signifier of a dubious quality called earn-
estness:

GWENDOLEN Ernest! My own Ernest! I felt from the first
   that you could have no other name!
JACK Gwendolen, it is a terrible thing for a man to find
   out suddenly that all his life he has been speaking
   nothing but the truth. Can you forgive me?
GWENDOLEN I can. For I feel that you are sure to change.[8]

The glibness of the resolution says that the age of miracles is past and
what remains is a joke. Shakespeare's comedy can also parody its own
conventions, but there is nothing glib about the ending of *Twelfth
Night*. The reappearance of Sebastian from 'his watery tomb' (5. 1. 232)
is the punch-line of a long drawn-out gag, but the gag does not
undermine the comedy's hope that 'Tempests are kind, and salt waves
fresh in love' (4. 1. 376). Wilde's Victorian comedy ends with a flurry of
embraces, since none of them matters very much. *Twelfth Night* ends
with a delay—'Do not embrace me till each cirumstance | Of place,
time, fortune do cohere and jump | That I am Viola' (5. 1. 249–51)—and
reminders of unfinished business.

   Shakespeare's comedies draw a large circle. So many pairs of lovers
crowd into it at the end of *As You Like It* that it looks to Jaques as if
'There is sure another flood toward, and these couples are coming to
the ark' (5. 4. 35). *Twelfth Night* brings in Toby and Maria to join Viola
and Orsino and Olivia and Sebastian. Some couples, like the silent
Isabella and Vienna's Duke, strain the limits of containment. Some are
uncomfortable being there, like Shylock's daughter Jessica and her

husband Lorenzo. Some characters, like Lucio in *Measure for Measure*, are desperate to get out; some, like Proteus in *The Two Gentleman of Verona*, may not deserve to be in. But however large it is, every circle defines an outside as well as an inside. The satirical Jaques leaves the other characters to their 'pleasures; | I am for other than for dancing measures' (5. 4. 190–1). Sebastian's loving friend Antonio in *Twelfth Night*, and the other solitary Antonio, who stakes his life for Bassanio in *The Merchant of Venice*, are onlookers from the margins of the circle. And then there are the characters who are excluded entirely from the betrothals, reunions, and reconciliations. Some are more noticeable by their absence than others. Paroles in *All's Well* and the villainous Don John in *Much Ado* can be left out on the ancient principle of getting what you deserve. But Shylock, by the power of his presence, becomes equally powerful in his absence. Technically, the Jew is a blocking-character; he is there to provide a resistance which has to be overcome so that Act 5 doesn't follow too quickly from Act 1. But his dramatic claim on us shows the losses as well as the gains that the genre entails.

Malvolio is another blocking-character. As steward he has a job to perform: he keeps the accounts, locks the doors, stops the music. But it is less Malvolio's repressiveness that gets him in trouble than his expansive desire to marry upward and become 'Count Malvolio'. Shakespearian comedy is tolerant of much; to a surprising degree, for instance, it tolerates an unsettling of gender boundaries. It is not equally tolerant of an unsettling of class boundaries. Malvolio's dream of upward mobility makes him a test-case of comedy's limits. From inside the comic circle, Malvolio looks like a power-hungry, self-loving antagonist of the carnival spirit. From outside, in terms either of social space or historical time, he may claim sympathy as the bourgeois victim of aristocratic exclusivity. Other characters reach out to Malvolio: 'Pursue him, and entreat him to a peace' (5. 1. 376), but their stage isn't big enough to hold him. Malvolio is no longer in yellow stockings and cross-gartered, and he is not smiling. He is in his customary suits of solemn black, and he has vowed 'I'll be revenged on the whole pack of you' (5. 1. 374). When he appears again it will not be in a comedy, and the setting will not be courtly Illyria but the cold, tragic castle of Elsinore.

History

BETWEEN comedy and tragedy in the Shakespeare Folio of 1623 comes history. It is a suggestive arrangement but, like the individual plays within the category, capable of suggesting competing possibilities. Does history bridge the distance between comedy and tragedy, drawing on the conventions of both? Or is history what separates comedy from tragedy, the intrusive world of 'real' events which turns comedy's dream of renewal into tragedy's anxious recognition of limitation ? Or does the placement of history signify nothing more than the editors' knowledge that most of Shakespeare's tragedies were written later than most of his histories? The question of where history comes on a map of the genres is only one of many questions that bedevil what you might think is the least questionable of Shakespeare's genres. Things happen, and history is the record of them, so Shakespeare's history plays belong to the genre in which the playwright tells it like it was—except that a moment's thought reveals the total inadequacy of that commonsense proposition. In the narratives of history, whether written by a playwright or a professional academic historian, the things that happen are given a shape and a meaning. The words 'history' and 'story' derive from the same root: we might say that history is a story which saves the past from the chaos of unmeaning events. The telling makes all the difference, since the same things can be made to tell more than one story, can make more than one kind of sense. The stories history tells are the record of the tellers' search for patterns and meanings, for causes and effects, origins and outcomes. And just as stories belong to various genres, so history too draws upon a variety of different generic conventions.

The plays Heminges and Condell grouped together as histories deal with a tiny sliver of the past. They deal mainly with the public realm, with political events, and specifically with the things that happened to or because of a few English kings. They draw their plots from a variety of sources, but primarily from several non-dramatic 'chronicles' of English history written during the Tudor period, from Henry VII to Queen Elizabeth. The chronicles helped create a new sense of an English nation; they are patriotic as well as scholarly works, recasting many different stories about dynastic turmoil into a saga of national and monarchical destiny. Shakespeare's dramatic appropriation of the chronicles was astonishingly original: it would be only a small exaggeration to say that 'history play' is the only genre he actually invented. Most earlier plays that could in the loosest sense be called 'history plays' look very little like Shakespeare's. The Protestant polemicist John Bale, in the early sixteenth century, wrote what has sometimes been called the first English history play, *King Johan* (the same King John that Shakespeare would write about); but Bale's play is a mixed-morality, in which King Johan and other historical figures appear on stage with a widow named England and a Catholic troublemaker named Sedition, and there is little room for ambiguity of motive or complexity of audience response. Shakespeare's contemporary Robert Greene wrote *James IV* (1590), a fantastic comical romance which has as much to do with Oberon, King of the Fairies, as it does with the historical Scottish king of its title. *The Famous Victories of Henry V*, an anonymous play from around 1588, was one of Shakespeare's sources for his own *Henry IV* and *Henry V*: it's a rollicking good show and, on its own terms, not a bad play; but in reworking the same material Shakespeare was in the process of discovering whole new ways of representing 'history'.

Very early in his career, probably between 1589 and 1594, Shakespeare wrote four related plays (a tetralogy) which the Folio calls *The First Part*, *The Second Part*, and *The Third Part of Henry the Sixth* and *The Life and Death of King Richard the Third*. They dramatize a troubled period, from the beginning of the reign of the child-king Henry VI (1422) to the overthrow of Richard III and the accession of Henry VII (1485), the first Tudor king and grandfather of Queen Elizabeth. It was the period which later historians called the Wars of the Roses, fought between the families of York and Lancaster for possession of the English crown. After the death of the Lancastrian Henry VI, the crown came to the Yorkist Edward IV; after Edward, it came to his brother, Richard III. Richard III was defeated at the battle of Bosworth by the forces of Henry Tudor, Earl of Richmond. Richmond's claim to the throne was based upon his descent from the House of Lancaster and solidified by his marriage to Elizabeth, eldest daughter of King Edward IV, of the House of York. As King Henry VII he united the families of York and Lancaster. Chronicle writers, in their function as propagandists, could claim that this progenitor of the Tudor monarchs gave legitimacy to the reigns of Henry VIII and his daughter, Queen Elizabeth.

Already we've got a pretty dense tangle of Henrys, Richards, Edwards, and Elizabeths. I urge the reader not to be frustrated: things are going to get worse. Because after Shakespeare finished this first tetralogy he wrote four other plays about English history which have, in the eyes of most critics, the appearance of a second tetralogy. Now he turned to events from the period preceding the historical sequence he had recently completed. The second tetralogy begins with *Richard II* and takes in the end of Richard's reign and his overthrow (1400) by Henry Bolingbroke; it continues with another period of civil war in *The First* and *The Second Part of Henry IV,* where the dominant dramatic figure is not the king but his son, Hal, the Prince of Wales; and it finishes in *Henry V* with England's victory over France and the king's marriage to the French princess Catherine, mother of Henry VI. In terms of historical sequence, the second tetralogy ends approximately where the first began.[1]

The First Folio groups two other plays among the histories. In *King John* Shakespeare moves back in time to the reign of a thirteenth-century monarch. He probably wrote it between the two tetralogies, although plausible arguments have also been made for an earlier date of composition. And very late in his career, after years occupied with tragedies and romances, he returned to English history with *Henry VIII*, written in collaboration with the playwright John Fletcher; the play concludes by prophesying the next stage in English history, the glorious reign of Elizabeth herself.[2]

But what about other plays based as firmly (or loosely) on what counted as 'history'? *King Lear*, *Macbeth*, and *Cymbeline* are plays about British monarchs, yet the Folio calls them 'Tragedies'. *Titus*

Andronicus, Julius Caesar, Coriolanus, and *Antony and Cleopatra* are drawn from the history of Rome, yet they too appear among the tragedies—while two of the plays grouped as 'Histories' in the Folio, *Richard III* and *Richard II,* are called tragedies on the title pages of their quarto editions. The overlapping and the apparently arbitrary inclusions and exclusions remind us again that a genre is not an ideal form laid up in heaven. The Folio's grouping of certain plays as 'Histories' is a response to the theatrical and political fashions of the time, which Shakespeare's plays fulfilled in the process of also remaking them. The history plays are a genre, but not in exactly the same way that comedy and tragedy are genres. Comedy and tragedy can be defined as genres on the basis of their respective dramatic forms; but as one critic writes, 'The history play cannot be defined on the basis of dramatic form, for the forms in which we find it are many.'[3] We could finesse the issue by saying that 'history' is only a sub-genre, a specialized instance of comedy or tragedy. Easier and more sensible is simply to assert that the history plays can be treated as a genre because playwrights and playgoers of the time did sometimes treat them that way; they wrote and responded on the basis of that understanding, with whatever difficulties that makes for later critics.

One difficulty is the special kind of relationship which the individual members of the genre bear to one another. Among the comedies we can find interesting connections between very different plays based on repeated motifs, character-types, structures of plot, and so on. The idea of genre allows us to recognize a relationship between such different roles as (say) that of Proteus in *The Two Gentlemen of Verona* and Bertram in *All's Well that Ends Well.* We recognize at least potential similarities between the partner-swapping in *A Midsummer Night's Dream* and the bed-tricks of *All's Well* and *Measure for Measure.* The history plays and their characters are related in those ways too, but they're related in the other sense of the word as well: King Henry V is the son of Henry IV and father of Henry VI. They may not appear in the same play (Henry VI has not been born by the time *Henry V* ends) but in a certain sense they exist for us simultaneously, because behind the discrete plot of each play there is another, longer plot. Watching *Henry IV* we remember the usurpation that took place in *Richard II;* and we remember it even if we haven't seen the earlier play, because the characters remember it. This is not simply a matter of strict historicity, of actual prior existence: Falstaff is a wholly invented character; he never appears on stage in *Henry V*; yet his existence in a previous play colours many of the events that happen in *Henry V.*

Which is to say that the history plays require a kind of double consciousness in the audience—of the individual play and of the longer historical narrative to which it refers. We can, as with the comedies or tragedies, think about types of characters. Shakespeare's kings tend to share their kingly traits (for instance, insomnia) because those traits belong to the genre as much as to the individual. We can think about motifs: images of gardens or pastoral retreats appear in each of the history plays, often as alternatives to the world of masculine competitiveness. But unlike the comedies and the tragedies, the individual history plays are thick with the memory or foreshadowing of one another. Events and characters literally live on beyond the boundaries of their individual plays, creating a sense of history as a densely interconnected world of stories told and retold, remembered and misremembered.

That density of interconnectedness, which is almost definitive of Shakespeare's achievement in the genre, is felt also in the range of characters. To say, with Sir Philip Sidney, that Shakespeare indecorously mixes clowns and kings is seriously to understate the matter. Common soldiers and their distressed wives, traders and farm labourers, a gardener, a waiter in a tavern, the groom who curries the king's horse, a country justice of the peace and his sleepy old cousin, a fat, boozy, decayed old aristocrat: the history that happens in these plays happens in a world more thickly imagined, more thoroughly populated with vividly recognized members of diverse social classes, than in any previous dramatic representation of history.

It is not only kings who have pasts and (if they're lucky) futures in Shakespeare's history plays. Richard II may bid his followers to 'sit upon the ground, | And tell sad stories of the death of kings' (3. 2. 151–2), but his storytelling is no more compelling than that of old Justice Shallow, in the sleepy calm of his country garden, recalling his long-ago days at the Inns of Court 'where I think they will talk of mad Shallow yet' (*2 Henry IV*, 3. 2. 13–14). King Richard's litany of dead kings is, if anything, less realized than Shallow's memories of 'little John Doit of Staffordshire, and black George Barnes, and Francis Pickbone, and Will Squeal, a Cotswold man'. The endless repetition of royal battles in the history plays engages our imaginations no more than Shallow's recollection of the day when the young Jack Falstaff broke 'Scoggin's head at the court gate': 'the very same day did I fight with one Samson Stockfish, a fruiterer, behind Gray's Inn. Jesu, Jesu, the mad days that I have spent! And to see how many of my old acquaintance are dead' (3. 2. 29–33). In *Henry V* the king cheers up his outnumbered army by creating, in advance, the myth of their future greatness, conjuring a time when each of the battle's survivors will 'stand a-tiptoe when this day is named', and 'strip his sleeve and show his scars | And say "These wounds I had on Crispin's Day"' (4. 3. 42, 47–8). It is a great image of national solidarity, but also powerful is the ghastly image of post-mortem solidarity imagined by a common soldier named Michael Williams, who thinks 'what a heavy reckoning' the king will make 'when all those legs and arms and heads chopped off in a battle shall join together at the latter day, and cry all, "We died at such a place"—some swearing, some crying for a surgeon, some upon their wives left poor behind them, some upon the debts they owe, some upon their children rawly left' (4. 1. 134–40). *All* those arms and legs, all the otherwise anonymous Toms and Dicks and Francises, even (because they are rare in the relatively masculine world of the history plays) all the wives, from Hotspur's Kate to Pistol's Doll: Shakespeare's imaginative fecundity peoples the world of his history plays in ways that are barely potential in his sources.

In the rest of this chapter I'll mainly be concerned with the two tetralogies; at the end of the chapter I'll turn briefly to *King John*. I begin by treating the plays roughly in order of composition, to recognize the diversity of their dramatic forms and to see how Shakespeare's conception of the genre changed from play to play. Only later will I consider what happens when we treat them as a connected group. At that point I'll ask some potentially contentious questions. Do the major history plays produce a unified vision of the period from Richard II to Henry VII? Does the genre construct a single explanation of English history? And if so, whose version of history is it?

The Two Tetralogies

The three parts of *Henry VI* are 'about' many things but they are not 'about' the character named King Henry VI in anything like the way

King Lear is about Lear or *Henry V* is about that 'star of England', King
Harry (*Henry V*, Epilogue 6). The plays teem with action and characters, some of whom take centre stage for a while, like the great
English warrior Talbot or Joan la Pucelle in Part 1, the rebel Jack Cade
or Queen Margaret in Part 2, or Richard, Duke of York (the future
Richard III) in Part 3; but none of them, and certainly not the
ineffectual Henry VI, dominates the action and gives it dramatic
shape. Certain moments stand out, especially those in which Shakespeare gives focus to the surrounding actions in an especially compact
dramatic image. In Part 1 the contentious Lancastrians and Yorkists
choose sides by plucking either a white rose or a red (the scene is a
Shakespearian invention rather than part of the existing historical
record), and Warwick makes the prophecy:

> this brawl today,
> Grown to this faction in the Temple garden,
> Shall send, between the red rose and the white,
> A thousand souls to death and deadly night.
> (*1 Henry VI*, 2. 4. 124–7)

Other such moments are more starkly symbolic. In Part 3, as civil war
rages, the pious King Henry moralizes about an ideal pastoral life that
would be spent watching the untroubled order of time, 'So minutes,
hours, days, weeks, months, and years, | Passed over to the end they
were created . . . Ah, what a life were this! How sweet! How lovely' (2.
5. 38–9, 41). Enter two soldiers, one who has unwittingly killed his
father, the other who has killed his son: ultimate emblems of the
disordered time of civil war. But such emblematic moments come
and go, as the characters come and go, in power or out, now alive
now dead, in plays that are pageant-like or episodic rather than
organized around either a single strong character or climactic event
(like the battle of Agincourt in *Henry V*). Moments and characters
echo one another; old wrongs are paid back with new wrongs. But the
plays do not build the tragic sense of a necessary beginning leading to a
dramatically inevitable end. Nor is there a comic sense that all the
complex tangle of action will right itself in a grand moment of self-
and social-discovery: the marriages in these plays are always part of the
problem, not the solution. The shape of history in the three parts of
Henry VI is forever changing—an incessant forming and reforming

and betrayal of alliances—and also curiously repetitive in its endless battles for power.

It is a way of staging history very different from that of Sackville and Norton's didactic historical tragedy *Gorboduc*, which we looked at in Chapter 2. *Gorboduc* has one point to make, about the dangers of divided rule, and it makes it repeatedly, with a chorus to underscore the dramatic issue in each act. *Gorboduc* was written for a courtly audience. The *Henry VI* plays, by contrast, were written for the public theatre, and were enormously popular in it. The three parts of *Henry VI* have something for everyone. There's the attractively energetic, crazily destructive lower-class revolutionary Jack Cade to make the audience's blood run cold. There are dangerous French women, like the witchy Joan or Queen Margaret, the 'she-wolf of France...an Amazonian trull' (*3 Henry VI*, 1. 4. 112, 115), to arouse masculine anxiety. There are treacherous Englishmen as well as heroic Englishmen—none more heroic or, on the Elizabethan stage, more popular than the great general, Lord Talbot, in *1 Henry VI*. Thomas Nashe, in 1592, writes about the hero's representation in the history play:

How would it have joyed brave Talbot, the terror of the French, to think that after he had lain two hundred years in his tomb, he should triumph again on the stage and have his bones new embalmed with tears of ten thousand spectators at least (at several times), who, in the tragedian who represents his person, imagine they see him fresh bleeding.[4]

Nashe's comment tells us much about the kind of play the audience saw. Talbot is 'represent[ed]' by a 'tragedian': whether or not the plays as a whole have the shape of Shakespearian tragedy, individual incidents in them affect the audience with the emotions appropriate to the sad deaths of the great. Most interesting in Nashe's account is the conflation of pride in country and pride in theatrical achievement. The living Talbot once struck terror into the enemy French; now the revived Talbot, 'fresh bleeding' on stage, draws a new army of English, ten thousand strong, into a communal experience, almost religious in nature, where the piteous spectacle of the hero's death converts the tears of grief into the preserving fluid of patriotic pride. In life Talbot was betrayed by his own countrymen; he was denied necessary reinforcements because of the 'jarring discord of nobility' (*1 Henry VI*, 4. 1. 188). But a united kingdom—united supposedly under Queen

Elizabeth and united in the theatre by its playwrights and actors—now gives Talbot new life, and finds in his represented death, not the spectacle of shameful power politics, but the redemptive image of English achievement. In Nashe's account, the history play performs a more than commemorative function; it redeems the past by turning its shames into current glory. When Talbot 'triumph[s] again on the stage', it is a triumph both for the nation, whose history is celebrated, and for the nation's theatre, the place pre-eminently where the dead bones of 'history' can live again.

With the emergence of Richard III (at the end of *3 Henry VI* and in the play that bears his name) Shakespeare begins to experiment with other forms of dramatic structure, other generic conventions. Richard is the first of Shakespeare's great self-fashioning characters. Sent before his time into the world scarce half made up (*Richard III*, 1. 1. 20–1), the shape-shifting Richard will make a virtue of necessity, counterfeiting the deep tragedian in his ability to impose his own will upon the stage of the world. *Richard III* is Richard's play in a way that the *Henry VI* plays are never quite Henry's. But it is not *only* Richard's play. For there is another script than the one he is in process of creating, one which at first contends with Richard's improvisation for possession of the stage and eventually banishes it; and in that script Richard is not the producing director but only 'a poor player | that struts and frets his hour upon the stage' (*Macbeth*, 5. 5. 23–4), unaware that all his gestures of actorly freedom have already been choreographed into a grander pageant over which he has no control. 'Since I cannot prove a lover', says Richard in his opening soliloquy (for once not giving himself sufficient credit), 'I am determinèd to prove a villain' (1. 1. 28, 30): 'determined', in the sense of having a strong personal intention, but also, unwittingly, 'determined' in the sense of being destined, as we might say that a life is determined from the start by heredity or the environment. Against Richard's daringly quirky voice are the play's other voices, those of the increasingly sizeable cast of his enemies, individually and in chorus pronouncing that Richard is not free, that the past is never gone, that 'history', far from being a mere succession of events, is a design, however indistinct at any given moment, always unfolding itself to reveal what it was always meant to be.

Behind the action hovers the old Queen Margaret, ritualistically pronouncing the symmetries of retribution:

I had an Edward till a Richard killed him;
I had a husband, till a Richard killed him.
(*To Elizabeth*) Thou hadst an Edward, till a Richard killed him;
Thou hadst a Richard, till a Richard killed him.

(4. 4. 40–3)

The play's machinery of ghosts and dreams and prophecies tells us that no action is without consequence. *Richard III* is a tragedy in the sense that the individual stories in *The Mirror for Magistrates* are tragedies: it dramatizes the rise and fall of an overweening individual. But it attributes his fall, not to the workings of cyclical fate, but to the relentless moral sensibility of his dramatic universe. The history of *Richard III* is purposive in a way that the earlier three histories are not; all Richard's self-inventions turn out to be stages on the way to the eventual appearance of his nemesis, Richmond, the future Henry VII. As dramatic character, Richmond is conspicuous by his absence; he is off-stage for most of the play and unimpressive when on. His triumph is less the triumph of an individual than the fulfilment of a foregone conclusion. The play's sense of a necessity fulfilled makes the crook-back Richard, for all the energy of his manic villainy, a kind of sacrificial victim.

In *Richard II*, the first play of the second tetralogy, Shakespeare returns to the idea of history's victim in a very different way. The difference, which has important consequences for the kind of play it is, can, in part, be attributed to the example of a history play by a different author. Christopher Marlowe's *Edward II* was probably written in 1592, shortly before the playwright's death. I called attention to this play, and to the mutual influence of Marlowe and Shakespeare, in Chapter 2. Here I'll isolate only two features that the plays share. The first is the dramatic conversion of a character's weakness into a sense of his pitiable victimization, so that his death can register as a tragic martyrdom. Both Marlowe's Edward II and Shakespeare's Richard II begin their plays as wilful, heedless monarchs, dedicated to fulfilling their own selfish desires rather than carrying out the difficult business of good government. Like the foolish kings of earlier mixed-morality plays, they ignore the good advice of wise counsellors and bring disaster upon themselves and their kingdom. But unlike those earlier type-figures, Edward and Richard become characters of great dramatic strength. The bad king becomes, as it were, a good victim, a tragic figure capable of eliciting an audience's sympathy rather than its moral scorn. Both Marlowe's king and Shakespeare's are stripped of their outward greatness; they are subjected to terrible indignities; and both discover, in their wretchedness, a powerful rhetoric of martyrdom which makes them dramatically stronger in defeat than they ever were in power.

The second, closely related feature is the creation of an idea of kingship not only as a public office or even as a gift from God, but as a heavy, a tragic, personal burden. In this rather odd construction of social fact, the king's greatness becomes inseparable from his sad vulnerability, with the result that kingship itself is invested with a peculiar kind of tragic glamour. So Marlowe's Edward, told that he should be patient in defeat, responds:

> The griefs of private men are soon allayed,
> But not of kings. The forest deer, being struck,
> Runs to an herb that closeth up the wounds,
> But when the imperial lion's flesh is gored,
> He rends and tears it with his wrathful paw,
> And highly scorning that the lowly earth
> Should drink his blood, mounts up into the air.[5]

Edward fluctuates between defiance and despair, and at both poles of his turmoil is the tragic fact of sacrificial kingship: 'But what are kings when regiment is gone, | But perfect shadows in a sunshine day?' (5. 1. 26–7).

In *Richard II*, Shakespeare echoes both the specific rhetoric and the larger dramatic logic of Marlowe's play. Richard's first response to Henry Bolingbroke's rebellion is to assert the king's special relationship to God:

> Not all the water in the rough rude sea
> Can wash the balm from an anointed king.
> The breath of worldly men cannot depose
> The deputy elected by the Lord.
> For every man that Bolingbroke hath pressed
> To lift shrewd steel against our golden crown,
> God for his Richard hath in heavenly pay
> A glorious angel. Then if angels fight,
> Weak men must fall; for heaven still guards the right.
>
> (3. 2. 50–8)

The irony is immediate: the next line brings news of Bolingbroke's victories. Obviously Richard is wrong about the precise nature of his relationship to God, but he is not so obviously wrong in claiming that there is a relationship. Explicitly he will compare himself to Christ and his enemies to Pontius Pilate. To be king, in Richard's rhetoric, is to be marked out for sacrificial death, 'for within the hollow crown | That rounds the mortal temples of a king | Keeps death his court' (3. 2. 156–8): it is the fate, he claims, of all kings, of legitimate monarchy itself; and by that token the king and the office of kingship become emotionally worthy of veneration.

Not, of course, that we have to give in to Richard's rhetoric. We can stand back from it and see its self-interested motive and try (if we think it worthwhile) to resist its emotional pull. Still, we have to recognize its consequences for the genre of *Richard II* and the other plays of the second tetralogy. The fall of a king becomes a special type of tragedy. It is not one which satisfyingly illustrates the workings of fortune's wheel but one which, in evoking the emotions of pity and fear, makes monarchs and monarchy—*English* monarchy of the recent historical past—at once glorious and imperilled, the more glorious for the peril. Dramatically it is a powerful idea but politically it has its problems, as no lesser an ideological critic than Queen Elizabeth recognized. When the Earl of Essex was preparing a coup d'état against her, his supporters paid Shakespeare's company to revive *Richard II*, not in order to evoke pity but to demonstrate that the breath of worldly men *can* depose a legitimate monarch. Elizabeth had no desire to become a victim, no intention of harvesting pity from defeat. It was not with aesthetic delight that she complained to the lawyer William Lambarde, 'I am Richard II. Know ye not that?'[6]

Richard dominates the last acts of his play, turning the victors into supporting players in the drama of his downfall. Even Bolingbroke— the future King Henry IV—is a dramatically dim figure compared to the Phaeton-like Richard. In the great scene of Richard's deposition (a scene which did not appear in editions of the play printed during Elizabeth's lifetime) Bolingbroke is, as Richard calls him, a 'silent King' (4. 1. 280), upstaged by the royal martyr acting his tragic script. Bolingbroke can 'seize the crown' (4. 1. 172), but he cannot so easily assume the mantle of legitimacy; he can take the worldly power, but not the aura of divinely sanctioned kingship. And in the next two plays of the second tetralogy, although the titles give him star billing, Henry IV remains a relatively dim figure, not silent but certainly not rhetorically commanding, as once again he is overshadowed, this time by his eventual successor, his own son, Prince Hal.

Again the dramaturgy is different from anything that had come before in the sequence of history plays, and produces a different idea of the genre's possibilities. But this time Shakespeare's manipulation of genre is truly revolutionary: nowhere in his career, nowhere in *any* playwright's career, is there a more daring, and successful, experiment in the possibilities of mixed dramatic kinds. Where Shakespeare's histories to this point have been so many variations on tragic forms and themes, the *Henry IV* plays are a virtual dialogue between tragedy and comedy. The biggest sign of this new departure is Falstaff. But the interplay between comedy and tragedy takes place not simply as the alternation of serious royal scenes with funny Falstaffian scenes. We see it in the opposing visions of life the characters represent; in, for instance, their relations to conceptions of Time itself, one of the variables of genre and the fundamental medium of history.

The first scene of Part 1 opens with an old man, 'wan with care', wishing he could find 'a time for frighted peace to pant' only in order to 'breathe short-winded accents' about new wars 'to be commenced in strands afar remote' (1. 1. 1–4). King Henry is a man on a treadmill: faced with incessant domestic strife he must keep on running as fast as he can simply to stay in the same place. If he could gather his disjointed kingdom together to 'march all one way' in a holy crusade 'as far as to the sepulchre of Christ', he could (he believes) leap off the treadmill of daily watchfulness into a grand sweep of fourteen hundred years of purposively organized time. That sweep of time began with Christ's crucifixion and, according to Henry, it leads directly to the England of his troubled reign; it makes everything that had come before in Henry's career, including his usurpation of the crown and the murder of Richard II, necessary steps on his redemptive road to Jerusalem. But Henry's 'purpose' (we immediately learn) 'is twelvemonth old'; and in the ten acts of the two parts of his play he will never 'find a time' that is not the tragic time of boundedness and self-defeat. His death will come approximately where he began, not in the Holy Land but in a room in Westminster called 'Jerusalem'; and all the aspirations of his reign will similarly be diminished by an inexorably tragic kind of time.

The second scene of Part 1 introduces us to another old man but a very different kind of time. 'Now, Hal, what time of day is it, lad?': the question is Hal's cue to define Falstaffian time, a medium measured not in unavailing battles and blows but in the gratification of appetitive desire:

What a devil hast thou to do with the time of the day? Unless hours were cups of sack, and minutes capons, and clocks the tongues of bawds, and dials the signs of leaping-houses, and the blessed sun himself a fair hot wench in flame-coloured taffeta, I see no reason why thou shouldst be so superfluous to demand the time of the day. (1. 2. 6–12)

Falstaff eats time and screws the instruments of its measurement. Unlike the King's linear time, Falstaff's time is a flexible medium. In it he can be as young as he wants ('They hate us youth!' (2. 2. 82–3)) or, when it suits his purpose, as old. He can be 'more valiant being, as he is, old Jack Falstaff' (2. 5. 482),[7] or he can even be dead Jack Falstaff, lying beside the corpse of Hotspur on the battlefield at Shrewsbury. But the stage direction tells us that Falstaff 'riseth up'— because you cannot keep this great tun of comic man down. In Part 1, Falstaff is the fleshy embodiment of comic immunity to the tragic laws of limit. In Part 2, however, the scene darkens and the comic routines grow tired. Now it becomes Falstaff's turn to learn what Hotspur, the valiant but doomed reaper of time's honours, discovered in Part 1, that 'time, that takes survey of all the world, | Must have a stop' (5. 4. 81–2). In Part 1 the joke is Falstaff's ability to avoid paying his debts; in Part 2 he is a man living on borrowed time, and his creditor is ready to call in the loan.

Between King Henry and Falstaff, then, stands Prince Hal. 'I know you all, and will a while uphold | The unyoked humour of your idleness' (Part 1, 1. 2. 192–3): Hal's declaration of intent defines his own special relationship to the medium of history. Biding his time with Falstaff and the tavern crew, he is also using time to secure his succession to a more stable throne: 'I'll so offend to make offence a skill, | Redeeming time when men think least I will' (Part 1, 1. 2. 213–14). Hal is neither a comic nor a tragic figure; he is the embodiment of a new idea of the royal agent of history, a new kind of hero for a new idea of history as a genre. From his sources Shakespeare inherited a complex, even contradictory, idea of the future King Henry V. In popular legend, preserved in the anonymous play called *The Famous Victories of Henry the Fifth*, Hal is a merry delinquent who suddenly undergoes a total personality change to become a great and wise ruler. In this version, the young Prince is whole-heartedly one of the tavern crew: 'We are all fellows, I tell you, sirs, and [if] the King | My father were dead, we would all be kings.'[8] When news of his father's sickness reaches him, this Prince declares that 'the breath shall no sooner be out of his mouth, but I will clap the crown on my head' (sc. 6, ll. 479–81). But the meeting with his father changes his mind—and his character—in an almost miraculous way: 'Even this day, I am born new again' (sc. 6, l. 581). But alongside this popular and comic myth, Tudor historians told a different story. The Prince of the chronicles is an astute power-player from the start; his father suspects that he is building his own popular base of support to force him into early retirement. Yet the historian's judgement is that, although 'he was youthfully given, grown to audacity, and had chosen him companions agreeable to his age', 'his behaviour was not offensive or at least tending to the damage of anybody, sith he had a care to avoid doing of wrong'.[9]

Shakespeare manages to have it both ways. Hal's first soliloquy clearly tells us that he knows exactly what he is doing and that his apparent dereliction is a politically shrewd act (the worse he appears now the better he'll look later). As a consequence, there is no change, not even much growth, in Hal's character throughout the two parts of *Henry IV*, because he is at the end exactly what he was at the start, a loyal son and a politically efficacious ruler-to-be. But many modern audiences, familiar with a different genre (the *bildungsroman*, or story of the growth of a young person towards a mature destiny) will not see it that way. Shakespeare allows the other (popular) version of Hal as the scapegrace youth to share the stage with this more cunning and unchanging Hal.

Hal has to be all things to all men so that he can stand at the centre of the amazing web of dramatic relationships Shakespeare constructs in *Henry IV*. At its simplest this is a matter of high and low: what happens in the royal scenes is mirrored in the comic tavern scenes. Hal's real father is the king, but in the tavern Falstaff plays the role of king and father. Henry owes the debts he incurred when he usurped Richard II's crown; Falstaff owes the hostess. And so on. The situation is complicated by a third locus of interest, the rebels and their leader, Hotspur. What Hotspur calls 'honour' King Henry calls rebellion and Falstaff calls a 'word' filled only with 'air'. King Henry wears a stolen crown, Hotspur wants to win a crown, Falstaff steals the coins called 'crowns'. Hal alone knows them all: literally he imitates or parodies each of these other players, and uses each of them to accomplish his goal. And as Shakespeare's Hal manages to be both the wild prince of popular legend and the thoughtful prince of the chronicler's history, so he manages to figure kingship both as a secular office secured by pragmatic, even Machiavellian, means and a sacred office authorized by God. At the beginning of Part 1, Hal claims that his delaying tactic is part of his plan for 'redeeming time' (1. 2. 214): the word suggests both a canny economic scheme to reap the profits from his invested time and a holy endeavour to deliver time from sin. Later he will tell his father that Hotspur is only his 'factor', an agent hired 'to engross up glorious deeds' until Hal chooses to call in the account: 'I will *redeem* all this on Percy's head . . . Or I will tear the *reckoning* from his heart' (3. 2. 132, 152, italics added). The 'reckoning' that is both a secular bill and a holy obligation is remembered throughout both parts of *Henry IV* in the density of references to debts, loans, and bills. Everyone, from the king to Falstaff to Francis, the overworked indentured drawer in the tavern, is pestered by indebtedness, both literal and figurative; and Hal is the kingdom's 'redeemer', its ultimate banker.

The vivid characters and the ingenious web of analogous actions in *Henry IV*, Parts 1 and 2, create a scene for history that has the spaciousness of the *Henry VI* plays but also the sharp focus of *Richard II*. Scenes which in the earlier history plays would have stood out as obviously emblematic Shakespeare here fully integrates with the surrounding action; and he makes scenes of low comedy inseparable from the high seriousness of royal history. Francis the harried tavern drawer, who can only say 'Anon' when Hal offers him freedom from his servitude, comically reflects Hotspur, whose self-defeating haste condemns him to be 'time's fool' (Part 1, 5. 4. 80); yet even the serviceable Francis has a dramatic life of his own. The scene in which Francis is the butt of Hal's practical joke is the same scene in which Hal and Falstaff, in their play extempore, successively 'stand for' the king. Their play-acting is ridiculous but also moving, as each man, playing a role, manages to speak the truth about their situation. 'Banish plump Jack, and banish all the world', is Falstaff's challenge; and Hal's answer, in his role as king, is breathtaking both in its directness and its emblematic force, 'I do; I will' (2. 5. 485–6).

The intricate structure of *Henry IV* has consequences for the kind of history it creates. As Shakespeare allows the double-faced word 'redeem' to suggest both a secular and a sacred transaction, so he figures the English monarchy itself as a kind of sacred business run by very human managers. The newly crowned King Henry V, at the end of *2 Henry IV*, is the successful product of his own public relations campaign; we see how Hal creates himself but we are nonetheless impressed by the creation. Falstaff too serves both to debunk and support royalty's special status: he is a satirist of royal pretensions but also a foil to make royalty shine brighter. In the kind of history Shakespeare creates in *Henry IV* there are no obviously right answers, no sharp demarcations of good guys from bad guys. The rejection of Falstaff is entirely justified and it is a callous, self-interested action. Hotspur is a blinkered rebel and a gallant knight. Hal is uneasy heir to a usurped throne and he is the time's redeemer.

Some critics who prize the teeming variety of *Henry IV* are disappointed by the more single-minded *Henry V*. The multivocality of *Henry IV*—all its differently compelling voices, coming from court or tavern or rebel camp, from nimble Falstaff to good, dull, honest Justice Shallow—is suppressed or dampened, as the Chorus literally tells us how we ought to respond. King Harry is 'the mirror of all Christian kings' (*Henry V*, Act 2 Chorus, 6); whoever beholds 'A little touch of Harry in the night' before the battle of Agincourt must 'cry "Praise and glory on his head!"' (Act 4 Chorus, 47, 31); for Harry is, the Chorus tells us, 'This star of England' (Epilogue, 6). Remnants of the dialogic structure of *Henry IV* remain but the differences are telling. Falstaff is absent from the play, except in the account of his off-stage death; and his lively tavern crew has diminished to the sick (and soon dead) Bardolph, the crazy Pistol, Nym, Mistress Quickly, and the boy who once served Falstaff. And Harry has virtually no contact with any of them (viewers of the Kenneth Branagh film adaptation may find this hard to believe). Disguised as 'Harry le Roy' he speaks a few words to Pistol, and he condemns an off-stage Bardolph to an off-stage death;

except for that, the play keeps a kind of *cordon sanitaire* between Harry and the tavern comics. And in place of those subversives it offers a new comic crew made up of the loyal representatives of a supposedly united kingdom, Jamie the Scotsman, Macmorris the Irishman, Gower the Englishman, and Fluellen, the wacky but loyal, always honourable Welshman. English traitors are soon exposed and, when exposed, literally thank God that they've been prevented from carrying out their evil designs. Even the enemy French, although they vastly out-number the English army, turn out to be pushovers; and their leaders, including the foppish, effeminate Dauphin and his aged father, are objects of ridicule, their very magnificence a sign of weakness in comparison to the bluff manliness of the English king and his beef-eating soldiers. In *Henry V* history is (apparently) a grand patriotic pageant which shows, according to King and Chorus, that God really is on the side of the English monarchy. (I say 'apparently' because, as we'll see, not all critics, from at least the nineteenth century, have been willing to do the Chorus's bidding and cry 'praise and glory' on King Harry's head.)

For its first four acts, *Henry V* is a play about men at war. But it ends with a marriage and with the trappings of a Shakespearian romantic comedy. King Harry and Princess Catherine belong to the company of Petruccio and Kate, Beatrice and Benedick: they are the odd couple who bicker their way to loving marriage. Their wooing in fractured French and English is a variation on the comedies' witty language of men and women punning their way to sexual union. We might be tempted to say that *Henry V* appends a comic resolution to an episodic history play. But the marriage is also a political act—a dynastic mar-riage—and for all its cuteness it is the final sign of the English king's victory. 'Wilt thou have me?', Harry asks Catherine; 'Dat is as it shall please de *roi mon père*', she responds, only to be assured 'Nay, it will please him well, Kate. It shall please him, Kate' (5. 2. 244–7). The comedy of Act 5, then, is not a sudden loosening of the historical reins in favour of comic licence, but the political conclusion to Henry V's effort to secure his title: 'No king of England', as he had said, 'if not king of France' (2. 2. 190). The romance of Act 5, with its imagery of fertile fields and masculine husbandry, is the sign that Henry V has won the peace that eluded his father and that he has, as promised, redeemed the time.

Chronicle History, Providential History, Shakespearian History

Except that the Epilogue to *Henry V* tells a different story. It acknowledges that Henry's peace was short-lived. After it came the reign of
the child-king Henry VI, with its civil wars and the loss of France,
'Which oft our stage hath shown' (Epilogue, 13). Thus the last play of
the second tetralogy ends by pointing us back to the earlier plays about
(the future) Henry VI. In doing so it explicitly raises a question about
how to view the plays. So far we have been looking at the diversity of
generic conventions Shakespeare calls upon in his history plays. We've
glanced from one play to the other, but mainly we've looked at each
play individually, as separate members of a loosely defined genre. But
what happens when we take the two tetralogies as a whole? Does the
multiplicity of conventions then cohere into a more clearly defined
genre which yields a single vision of English history?

Modern critics have given surprisingly diverse and contentious
responses to the question. E. M. W. Tillyard, in his influential *Shakespeare's History Plays* (1944), saw the two tetralogies as a unified story
which 'was nearly the same' as the story told by one of Shakespeare's
chronicle sources, Edward Hall's *Union of the Two Noble and Illustre
Families of York and Lancaster* (earliest surviving edition 1548).[10] Hall's
history has a moral: as Tillyard recounts it, Henry IV committed a sin
in usurping the throne and causing the death of Richard II; 'God
punished Henry [IV] by making his reign unquiet but postponed full
vengeance till a later generation' (60); God's vengeance was further
delayed in the next reign:

[But] with Henry VI the curse is realised and in the dreaded form of a child
being king . . . Meanwhile Providence is taking good care of Henry Tudor, Earl
of Richmond, and sees to it that he is out of the Yorkists' reach in Brittany.
. . . [Richmond unites the houses of York and Lancaster under God's providence.] In Henry VIII the process is complete, and his reign is triumphant.
(60–1)

This version of history, which Tillyard claims is Shakespeare's as well
as Hall's, has been called 'providential history'. It makes all that
happens (both for good and ill) part of God's plan, so that history is
neither a set of random events nor even, primarily, the product of
human actions but the inscription of divine providence. History con-

tains many tragic events but ultimately it has a happy ending, since it is the ending appointed by God.

There are problems with this as an account of the genre of Shakespeare's two tetralogies. It assumes that Shakespeare had the entire plan of the eight plays in mind when he began the first, and that in the decade of composition he never wavered from that plan. Drawing so heavily on Hall's chronicle, Tillyard by his own admission recounts a minority 'learned' view, which was also the official Tudor view of recent English history. There were other, competing ways of viewing the events Shakespeare dramatizes. While Tillyard refers to dissenting views he also claims that Hall's official Tudor account embodied a world-view that all right-minded Elizabethans believed. And Shakespeare becomes just such a right-minded Elizabethan. Finally, Tillyard chooses to elevate Hall's version of English history at the expense of the work Shakespeare drew on more extensively and pervasively, Raphael Holinshed's *Chronicles of England, Scotland and Ireland.*

The first edition of Holinshed's *Chronicles* appeared in 1578, but Shakespeare read the revised, expanded version of 1587. Holinshed was not the sole author of these enormous volumes. Holinshed compiled the work of various writers into what is in effect one gigantic committee report, which itself drew upon the work of previous chroniclers. Like any such report, it had to accommodate sometimes competing accounts of the same events. Holinshed is capable of admitting doubt about his sources or acknowledging that different sources offer different accounts. Where he cannot find a single coherent narrative, he allows the incoherence to stand. For recent critics, these traits are a virtue rather than the defects they were for Tillyard; they demonstrate a respect for the limits of historical certainty and a tolerance for divergent views.[11] Holinshed's acceptance of indeterminacy is more akin to Shakespeare's method in the history plays than is the simplifying clarity of Hall's narrative. This is not to say that Holinshed's history is radically different from Hall's—they agree on many fundamentals; but one difference in tendency is significant for our understanding of the genre of history Shakespeare wrote. Although Holinshed never questions the divine presence in human history, God's authorial hand is relatively less visible in his account than it is in Hall's.

Hall simplified and Holinshed complicated. Shakespeare, in a sense, did both: he dramatized. He reshaped his sources, inventing whole incidents and slews of characters, altering temporal sequence, mingling scenes of penetrating psychological portraiture with scenes of almost allegorical significance, to produce plays (each one significantly different from the other) so intricately designed that critics and audiences, all agreeing that there is a design, can disagree endlessly about its shape. *Henry V* is the most notorious case. For some, the play is essentially the play the Chorus asks us to see, a rousing patriotic pageant about 'the perfect mirror of all Christian kings'. For others it is an ironic exposure of a viciously Machiavellian prince, its meaning located precisely in the distance between what the all-praising Chorus says and what the scenes of war and political scheming show. One critic wittily describes the design of *Henry V* as a kind of optical illusion, like the drawing which looks either like a rabbit or a duck, depending on how you view it: the picture itself is in fact always both rabbit and duck, but the human eye can never see it as both simultaneously.[12]

The critical reception of *Henry V* is the extreme case. A more subtle example of Shakespearian complexity, in the reshaping of sources and in the shaping of his own play, can be mined from the last meeting between the Prince and his dying father in *2 Henry IV*. Here is Holinshed's account:

'Well, fair son (said the king with a great sigh) what right I had to [the crown], God knoweth.' [In the margin, Holinshed comments, 'A guilty conscience in extremity of sickness pincheth sore.'] 'Well (said the prince) if you die king I will have the garland, and trust to keep it with the sword against all mine enemies, as you have done.' 'Then', said the king, 'I commit all to God, and remember you to do well.' With that he turned himself in his bed, and shortly after departed to God in a chamber of the abbots of Westminster called Jerusalem...[13]

Small changes make large differences. Shakespeare makes Henry's confession—

> God knows, my son,
> By what bypaths and indirect crook'd ways
> I met this crown; and I myself know well
> How troublesome it sat upon my head.

> (4. 3. 312–15)

—a more poignant, almost weary acknowledgement that what God knows, Henry himself really may not know: motives and even the sequence of events have grown hopelessly complicated and beyond the human actor's ability to grasp.

And in Shakespeare's version, unlike Holinshed's, the king tells Hal about his plan 'To lead out many to the Holy Land'. This private communication differs significantly from his public statement of a redemptive mission at the opening of *1 Henry IV*. Now Henry describes the expedition as a pragmatic, politically motivated plan to turn his enemies' attentions outward to a common enemy, 'Lest rest and lying still might make them look | Too near unto my state' (4. 3. 340–1). The father advises his son to keep up the good work:

> Therefore, my Harry,
> Be it thy course to busy giddy minds
> With foreign quarrels, that action hence borne out
> May waste the memory of the former days.
>
> (341–4)

In Holinshed, the Prince says only that he will keep the royal 'garland' 'with the sword against all mine enemies'. Shakespeare's Hal has more ambitious plans, not only to keep but to legitimize his possession of the crown:

> My gracious liege,
> You won it, wore it, kept it, gave it me;
> Then plain and right must my possession be,
> Which I with more than with a common pain
> 'Gainst all the world will rightfully maintain.
>
> (4. 3. 349–53)

But 'plain and right' is hardly an accurate summary of the political and dramatic situation. On the one hand, Shakespeare seems to give fuller justification for the legal basis of the future Henry V's reign in the claim that lineal descent of the crown, however it was originally won, makes the 'possession' of it rightful. On the other hand, he invites us to ask how maintaining a wrong can ever convert that wrong to right. Hal, who makes the claim, knows the problem better than anyone. In *Henry V*, immediately before the battle of Agincourt, the almost-panicky king begs God to 'think not upon the fault | My father made in compassing the crown', and acknowledges that his 'penitence comes after ill, | Imploring pardon' (4. 2. 290–1, 301–2).

A providentialist reading of the two tetralogies can go a long way towards reconciling apparent contradictions: Henry V's claim to the throne is justified because it is part of God's long-term plan, even if his claim does not resolve the legitimacy issue that began with Henry IV's usurpation. But a providentialist view of the two tetralogies as a single story with an eventually triumphant shape requires a very distant view; it focuses on the supposedly grand design, and in the process it may pay less attention to the up-close details of individual plays, where motives, actions, and outcomes are resistant to any single or totalizing explanation.

Historians, like dramatists, sometimes create stories in which a clear right opposes a clear wrong. Less common but more interesting is the kind of conflict Shakespeare favours in his history plays, in which two rights clash and neither side is exclusively good or bad. His dramatized conflicts of competing rights can even call in question the absoluteness of the categories right and wrong, good and bad. Is it ever right to disobey a legitimate monarch? A question, as Falstaff might say, not to be asked. The unified authority of church and state drummed into the ears of Shakespeare's contemporaries an unequivocal message about obedience to authority. Queen Elizabeth ordered that *An Homily Against Disobedience and Wilfull Rebellion* should be preached annually from all the pulpits in the country. It said that 'Obedience is the principal virtue of all virtues, and indeed the very root of all virtues, and the cause of all felicity', while disobedience is literally the original sin, 'both the first and greatest, and the very [root] of all other sins, and the first and principal cause both of all worldly and bodily miseries, sorrows, diseases, sicknesses, and deaths, and which is infinitely worse than all these, as is said, the very cause of death and damnation eternal also.'[4] Which is pretty absolute, until one looks at actual cases. Once upon a time, the Pope was absolutely to be obeyed. But the queen's own father, King Henry VIII, disobeyed the Pope and made himself head of the church in England; and now the rebel English church preached the doctrine of absolute obedience to English royal authority. Confusing? Not to a Protestant historian who believed that the Pope's authority was usurped rather than derived originally from God. All you need to know in order to be obedient is who has the legitimate right to be obeyed. If there is only one claimant, you might take it on trust; but Shakespeare's history plays show that there is always more than one. The historical record is the basis of authority, but that record (the narrative of the past on which present legitimacy rests) is exactly what rival claimants incessantly fight over.

In *1 Henry VI* the Wars of the Roses seem to begin over a legal technicality: was the father of Richard Plantagenet 'attached' or 'attainted' as a traitor? On that distinction hinges Plantagenet's right to succeed to the title of Duke of York. Since the disputants disagree about the historical facts, they choose sides and fight. In *Henry IV* Lord Mortimer (Richard II's own choice to succeed) has a nearer lineal claim than Henry, who is the crowned king by right of possession. Which historical right, of actual possession or of lineage, should prevail? At the battle of Shrewsbury the royalist forces adopt a common military tactic: King Henry sends out several of his commanders wearing his royal insignia so that the enemy, unable to recognize the real king, will not know where to mass their forces. 'The king hath many marching in his coats' says Hotspur (*1 Henry IV* 5. 3. 25): a statement not only about military tactics but about how easily the 'gorgeous garment, majesty' (*2 Henry IV*, 5. 2. 44) can be put on or taken off, despite the supposedly iron claim of lineal descent. The kings and would-be kings of Shakespeare's history plays are constantly in search of a history that would justify their present and their future. In Act 1 of *Henry V* the king asks the Archbishop of Canterbury whether he has a legitimate claim to rule in France. The Archbishop produces a long-winded historical account of the so-called Salic law that proclaims 'No woman shall succeed in Salic land' (1. 2. 39). Henry's own claim rests on the female line. But what is 'Salic land'? Does it refer to France or Germany? The search for historical justification leads the churchmen back 420 years to 'the defunction of Pharamond', and through a litany of rulers and claimants so long and complicated that by its end we hardly know whether Shakespeare intends this as a serious interpretation of history or a satire on a politician's use of history to establish the legitimacy of his claims.

Only a villain—a smart, eloquent villain, like the bastard Edmond in *King Lear*—would claim that 'legitimate' is only a 'fine word' or that law itself is merely 'the plague of custom' (F, 1. 2. 18, 3) made by some people to keep other people in their place. The vast propaganda resources of the Elizabethan state, and then, even more ferociously, of the Jacobean state, were dedicated to the proposition that the monarch's law was the local habitation of God's law and that God stands up not, as Edmond prays, for bastards but for the 'legitimate'. God made the law that makes an English monarch—a proposition with which Shakespeare's Richard II agrees: 'The breath of worldly men cannot depose | The deputy elected by the Lord' (*Richard II*, 3. 2. 52–4). That is Richard's bold claim, one short act before he gives the crown's 'heavy weight from off [his] head' and with his own tears washes away his balm (4. 1. 194, 197). History records the uncontested facts that Richard II was a legitimate king and that Richard II was deposed. Out of those apparently irreconcilable facts Shakespeare constructs a play that does not decide the questions (is God on Richard's side? should subjects ever take the law into their own hands?) but makes the problem of answering them integral to its generic form.

King John

King John, which falls outside the sequence of the two tetralogies, poses the issue of legitimacy in a particularly demanding way. And it increases our sense of the diversity of Shakespeare's idea of history as a dramatic genre.

To the Protestant chroniclers of Tudor England, King John was one of history's heroes because, like Henry VIII three centuries later, he defied the power of the Pope. Shakespeare not only toned down the anti-Catholicism of his sources; he made it entirely unclear whose side God would be on were he to be on anyone's side in the dynastic and international conflicts of John's reign. As his own mother says, John maintains his throne by 'strong possession much more than . . . right' (1. 1. 40): in the line of succession from John's brother Richard Coeur-de-lion, the 'right' belongs to John's nephew, the child Arthur. It is a no-win situation for monarchical stability: strict legitimacy argues in favour of Arthur's right, but to overthrow John would be like allowing the rebels to defeat Henry IV.

That difficult situation is only part of the reason that modern audiences and readers find *King John* a confusing or, indeed, a confused play. We have trouble reading its generic codes: we recognize conventions that are familiar to us from the other history plays, but we have difficulty seeing a consistent pattern in their deployment. And why not? The figure who establishes the closest relationship with the audience—who speaks to us in soliloquy, gives the most trenchant commentary on the action, and finally has the play's last patriotic word— is a figure known as the Bastard. Illegitimacy is not an abstract issue in *King John* but a central character, possibly a hero.

The Bastard (Philip Faulconbridge, an unacknowledged son of Coeur-de-lion) is himself a compound of potentially conflicting generic properties. He has the makings of a kind of folkloric hero, the 'natural' son of a king with all his father's royal spirit but unconstrained by social convention. He is a witty rogue, almost at times Falstaffian in his apparent contempt for false piety and the hypocrisy of statecraft. But his sense of humour can have a grim, even a grotesque edge to it— an edge that makes him, at times, a Vice-figure or (the figure's later incarnation) a Machiavellian, as when he urges a temporary alliance between John's side and Arthur's so that together they can destroy the town of Angiers before getting back to fighting each other. He is a satirist who can see through the high-flown claims of politicians to the self-interest, or as he calls it 'commodity', that governs their actions. But his satirical indignation can also be a cynical ambitiousness that makes him little different from the objects of his scorn: 'Since kings break faith upon commodity, | Gain be my lord, for I will worship thee' (2. 1. 599). The worship of 'commodity' reminds us of that other bastard, Edmond, in *King Lear*, with his worship of the vicious goddess 'Nature'. *King John*'s Bastard has a prickly self-defensive pride ('I am I, howe'er I was begot' (1. 1. 175)), like Edmond's ('I should have been that I am had the maidenliest star in the firmament twinkled on my bastardizing' (F, 1. 2. 128–30)). But *King John*'s Bastard is a true-blue patriotic Englishman; and at the end, after John's death and the succession of John's son, he sounds less like the selfish Edmond than like the prophetic John of Gaunt in *Richard II*:

> This England never did, nor never shall,
> Lie at the proud foot of a conqueror
> But when it first did help to wound itself
>
> . . . . .
> Naught shall make us rue
> If England to itself do rest but true.
>
> (5. 7. 112–14, 117–18)

It's a rousing conclusion to a play in which the illegitimate son of a legitimate king has been loyal throughout to a king (John) whose claim to the English throne is a never-resolved point of contention.

Shakespeare's audience, familiar with the conventions Shakespeare is drawing upon, might have had less trouble than we do making the Bastard's character satisfyingly coherent. (Or they might have had a higher tolerance for conventions of character that allowed a complexity we can only see as incoherence.) But they might also have had less trouble with the play precisely because they did *not* yet know the full sweep of the two tetralogies. From *Richard III* we expect John's history to have a certain sense of doom-laden destiny hanging over it; but the play is in fact resolutely secular in that regard, and presents accidents (for instance, the death of young Arthur) as no more than accidents. The rhetoric of kingship's sacred character, so prominent in the second tetralogy, is almost entirely absent from *King John*. And by playing down both the wickedness of the Pope and the goodness of John in defying him, Shakespeare deprives the play of a certain kind of historical momentousness available in his sources. *King John* seems an oddity among the history plays partly because we know what Shakespeare was to make out of the genre in later plays—but those later plays are, no less than *King John*, experiments in the diverse possibilities available to an author who both uses and stunningly revises the resources of a genre's traditions.

5

Tragedy

'Boy Killed in Tragedy', the headline reads, and I buy the paper, expecting to find the review of a play. To my disappointment I find that the story has nothing to do with plays or genres. Instead it's a report about a little boy whose bike veered into the path of a passing bus. The child died instantly. And even I, despite my reprehensibly narrow interests, get the point. What more horrible thing can we imagine than the absolutely unprepared, unprovoked, violent death of a child? True, the Greek word *tragoedia* referred to a kind of drama long before it was extended to events in real life: etymologically, the boy's real death is a 'tragedy' because it is like the sort of thing that might happen in a tragic play; and true too that the randomness of this real-life tragedy is worlds apart from the dramatic inevitability which Aristotle required in the best Greek tragedies. 'Boy Killed in Tragedy' is an example of life imitating art, and doing it badly. But the newspaper article does share one thing with Shakespearian tragedy: where tragedy is, death is too; and when the final death has happened, the tragedy is complete.

But everyone dies. If death were all that tragedy required, then tragedy would be, to use Hamlet's word, as 'common' as dirt. Yet tragedy, although it presents the single absolutely universal fact of life, is, compared to comedy, the rarer form. Comedy, which is dedicated to the avoidance of death, has thrived during periods (including our own) when tragedy lacked a cultural environment which was conducive to the production of enduringly stage-worthy plays. But if tragedy is the minority form it is, by the same token, the more prestigious; yet this not only because of the devastating truth it tells. 'Now get you to my lady's chamber', says Hamlet, holding the skull of Yorick, 'and tell her, let her paint an inch thick, to this favour she must come' (5. 1. 188–90). The message delivered by Yorick's rotting skull is, in itself, banal: we know that all life ends in death. Why seems it, as Gertrude asks Hamlet about his father's death, so particular to him? Why should certain presentations of the 'common' fact of human mortality seem so utterly remarkable, so searingly 'particular'? Gertrude's question is a fundamental question about Shakespearian tragedy.

According to the table of contents in the First Folio, Shakespeare wrote more comedies than tragedies. The Folio lists eleven tragedies, but it includes *Cymbeline* among those eleven: most critics agree that this is just an editorial accident. But there are other ways of cutting up the canon. Twenty-five years before the First Folio, Francis Meres, in *Palladis Tamia*, made the first list we have of Shakespeare's plays. Unlike Heminges and Condell's Folio, which made 'history' one of three Shakespearian kinds, Meres divided the dramatic kingdom in two. Four of the plays that Heminges and Condell called histories, Meres called tragedies. For Meres, writing in the first years of Shakespeare's career, Shakespeare's already assured greatness as a tragic writer was based on *Richard II, Henry IV, Richard III, King John, Titus Andronicus*, and *Romeo and Juliet*. Meres does not have to explain his criteria for including the plays about English kings: clearly they deal with 'majestical matters', they present the misfortunes of great men, they are (as both Aristotle and Horace recommended) based on stories already known to the audience, and for all their internal variety they do at times climb to an elevated, a tragic, style.

In fact, the definition of Shakespeare's tragic canon has never been stable, because the definition of tragedy, as a genre, has not been stable. We have seen that Sir Philip Sidney, writing immediately before Shakespeare, could find no English play he considered a 'right' tragedy. With the partial exception of *Gorbuduc*, which at least had a tragic style, all the English plays Sidney knew violated the 'precepts' of time and place and they all thrust in clowns to play a part in majestical matters. From Sidney's perspective, none of Shakespeare's plays would be 'right' tragedies. And at the beginning of the twentieth century, A. C. Bradley, in his enormously influential book *Shakespearian Tragedy* (1904), was only slightly less exclusive in defining what he considered Shakespeare's 'pure tragedies'. His definition is thematic or philosophical rather than formal. He asks,

What is the substance of Shakespearian tragedy, taken in abstraction both from its form and from the differences in point of substance between one tragedy and another? Or...what is the nature of the tragic aspect of life as represented by Shakespeare? What is the general fact shown now in this tragedy and now in that?[1]

To find the answer, Bradley 'abstracts' and excludes much of what we have included in our own discussion of Shakespeare's genres: 'Nothing will be said either of Shakespeare's place in the history of English literature or of the drama in general. No attempt will be made to compare him with other writers.' There will be no attention to his 'development' or to his 'sources, texts, [or] the interrelations of his various works' (p. xi). And several of those works will be discounted. *Romeo and Juliet* may be a 'pure tragedy' but it is 'an immature one'; *Richard III, Richard II, Julius Caesar, Antony and Cleopatra*, and *Coriolanus* 'are tragic histories or historical tragedies', which owe too much to their sources 'to be judged by the standard of pure tragedy'; *Titus Andronicus* lacks Shakespeare's 'characteristic tragic conception', and much of *Timon of Athens* should (Bradley thinks) 'be attributed to some other writer'. We are left with *Hamlet, Othello, King Lear*, and *Macbeth*. Bradley did not invent this distinction between the Big Four and all the rest, but he gave it an authority which still shapes, or distorts, our notion of Shakespearian tragedy as a whole.

My own interest in this chapter will not be in any essence of 'right' or 'pure' tragedy, but precisely in the generative combinations that make up the range of Shakespeare's practice. I favour the Folio's division but I will draw on the other contenders when appropriate. With the two exceptions of *Titus Andronicus* and *Romeo and Juliet*, the plays designated as tragedies in the Folio were probably all written after 1598. Throughout Shakespeare's life to that point, England had known only one monarch, Queen Elizabeth. Now the queen was old, and her refusal to name an heir, which had for long been a successful political gambit, was making the uncertainties of royal succession a consuming national interest. So the chronology of Shakespeare's career, which makes his most intense involvement with tragedy coincide with the period of transition from Elizabeth's reign to King James's, is worth keeping in mind: it suggests why the line (as Heminges and Condell draw it) between tragedy and history plays is sometimes worth crossing. Other lines, too, draw themselves only in order to be redrawn. For some purposes we can distinguish the 'Roman plays'—*Titus Andronicus, Julius Caesar, Coriolanus, Antony and Cleopatra*—as a group, although they go from earliest to latest in Shakespeare's chronology. For some purposes we can pair *Titus Andronicus* with the very different *Hamlet* as so-called 'revenge tragedies'; for other purposes we can group both plays along with *King Lear* and *Macbeth* as plays about dynastic succession. *Titus, Hamlet*, and *Lear* are plays about parents and children, as are *Romeo and Juliet* and even *Coriolanus*, whose title-character tries to 'stand | As if a man were author of himself | And knew no other kin' (5. 3. 35–7). Shakespeare, like some of his contemporaries, sometimes disregarded the criterion of 'majestical matters': *Romeo and Juliet* and *Othello* are, in their very different ways, 'domestic tragedies'. Yet *Antony and Cleopatra*, whose protagonists are as majestic as they come, is, like *Romeo and Juliet* and *Othello*, a lovers' tragedy. The groups form and reform themselves and in the process baffle attempts to create a single scheme. So we'll cast the net widely—taking in, on occasion, even the final romances or, as Shakespeare might have called them, tragicomedies—in order to recognize the variety of Shakespeare's experimentation with the genre.

Most of the plays we think of as tragedies have at their dominating centre a single remarkable protagonist—except that *Romeo and Juliet, Antony and Cleopatra*, and, arguably, *Macbeth* are about remarkable pairs of protagonists. Or should we call them heroes and heroines? Those designations imply moral judgements and involve us in debates about what is or isn't heroic about a character. Richard III and Macbeth are villains by any standard, as they themselves well know. But most of Shakespeare's tragic characters are a morally mixed lot. Is Hamlet, who causes so many deaths, a 'sweet prince', a divine avenger, or a philosophical killer? He has been played as all of these and more. Othello is one of Shakespeare's most sympathetic characters, and he is also a murderer. Lear, towering in his demands for justice, is at the same time a monster of over-bearing selfishness. Brutus is a high-minded republican and a self-deluded pawn in the power struggle against a ruler, Caesar, who eludes our judgement as much as Brutus himself does. The love of Antony and Cleopatra is beyond reckoning; they make death proud to take them. Yet along with their greatness, we can see Antony as 'a strumpet's fool' (1. 1. 13); and beneath the gorgeous folds of Cleopatra's rhetoric there was visible, on Shakespeare's stage, a 'squeaking' actor 'boy[ing her] greatness | I'th' posture of a whore' (5. 2. 216–17).

So let that be one generalization about Shakespeare's tragedies: they present, not moral examples of goodness or wickedness but mixed characters whose greatness is inextricable from the things that undermine it. Other ideas will follow from this. We'll notice in many of Shakespeare's tragic characters a degree of self-awareness beyond anything his immediate antecedents in the genre could prepare us for; and we'll notice the development of a language to express, or create, that psychological awareness. (Moralistic judgements on Shakespeare's characters often sound shoddy because the characters have already judged themselves more trenchantly than we can. The so-called 'tragic flaw', a modern invention based on a misreading of Aristotle, is a reductive moralizing of what the characters often know more complexly about themselves.) Linked to tragic self-consciousness is a consciousness of the social or divine economies which limit, as they also in part define, the self: we'll notice the tragic struggle between individual autonomy and some shaping force (providence, fate, the stars, the gods, nature, even *theatre*) which limits that autonomy. And we'll notice that each of these generalizations about tragedy could also apply to comedy, where (for instance) characters also try to assert an autonomy which the plot sometimes gleefully denies them. So in discussing one genre we must keep the other in mind as well. Shakespearian tragedy is not the opposite (whatever that would mean) of Shakespearian comedy. The kinds depend upon or imply one another. There are many ways to express their relationship; one of the most intriguing is Northrop Frye's observation that 'tragedy is really implicit or uncompleted comedy, [and] comedy contains a potential tragedy within itself'.[2]

Tragic Characters: Freedom and Design, Revenge and Repentance

'The pity of it': what Othello in his delusion says of Desdemona's supposed infidelity could be said of his own history and that of other Shakespearian tragic characters. In this conception of tragic character, where a murderer can elicit sympathy as much as a pair of star-crossed teenage lovers, Shakespeare is, in part, responding (as he did in the history plays) to the formative example of Christopher Marlowe.

Marlowe's Faustus in his overweening search for intellectual and
temporal power sells his soul to the devil: he wills his own damnation.
Yet our response is not the satisfaction that comes from knowing he
got what he deserved. Moments of startling self-knowledge strike
through the moral madness of Faustus's actions, making his life
and death the occasion for our pity as well as for our fear of God's
justice:

> What art thou, Faustus, but a man condemned to die?
> Thy fatal hour draws to a final end.
> Despair doth drive distrust into thy thoughts.
> Confound these passions with a quiet sleep.
> Tush! Christ did call the thief upon the cross;
> Then rest thee, Faustus, quiet in conceit.
>
> (4. 5. 33–8).[3]

Here, Faustus comforts himself with a false hope—and knows it is a
false hope ('conceit'); and sleepily he returns to the sensual enjoyment
of his own damned condition. In the last accelerated hour of his life
Faustus cries out confusedly to both God and Lucifer:

> O, I'll leap up to my God! Who pulls me down?
> See, see, where Christ's blood streams in the firmament!
> One drop would save my soul, half a drop! Ah, my Christ!
> Rend not my heart for naming of my Christ!
> Yet will I call on him. O, spare me, Lucifer!
>
> (5.2.142–6)

But neither God nor Lucifer will spare this man whose greatness and
folly we have seen so vividly realized. A final Chorus tries to impose a
neat didacticism on the play:

> Regard his hellish fall,
> Whose fiendful fortune may exhort the wise
> Only to wonder at unlawful things,
> Whose deepness doth entice such forward wits
> To practice more than heavenly power permits.

But the play has generated energies which cannot be contained by that
warning. We are as likely 'to wonder' at the implacable deity who
demands Faustus's endless suffering as we are to applaud the destruction of Faustus's attempt to conquer the universe with his aspiring
mind.

Faustus is an extreme case. And Shakespeare never dealt so explicitly with theology as Marlowe does in his revisionary version of medieval allegory. In the early *Richard III*, however, the tension between individual aspiration and an impersonal order that constrains individuality is almost schematically vocalized in the contrast between Richard's wry and wily speech and the symmetrically formal speeches of his increasingly numerous enemies. The Richard who emerged in *3 Henry VI* takes, as we saw in Chapter 2, wicked pleasure in his own inventiveness: 'Can I do this and cannot get a crown? | Tut, were it farther off I'll pluck it down!' (3. 2. 194–5). In *Richard III* that jaunty delight in overcoming difficulty continues as the misshapen Richard woos the widow of the man he has just killed. No one is more amazed by his success than Richard:

> Was ever woman in this humour wooed?
> Was ever woman in this humour won?
> I'll have her, but I will not keep her long.
>
> .   .   .   .   .
>
> Upon my life she finds, although I cannot,
> Myself to be a marv'lous proper man.
>
> .   .   .   .   .
>
> Shine out, fair sun, till I have bought a glass,
> Where I may see my shadow as I pass.
> (1. 2. 215–50)

The wooing itself has the kind of quick verbal give-and-take which, in comedy, makes lovers of antagonistic odd-couples. Richard's wooing shows another, darker possibility for a similar technique. And in Richard's *next* wooing—this time of the mother of his next intended bride—we again hear an almost-comic repartee, except that this time the dialogue's rhythm expresses not inventive freedom but an implacable destiny closing in on the beleaguered Richard. He tries to swear his good intentions but his interlocutor successively disables every pledge:

> RICHARD   Now by my George, my garter, and my
>   crown—
> ELIZABETH   Profaned, dishonoured, and the third
>   usurped.
> RICHARD   I swear—
> ELIZABETH   By nothing, for this is no oath.
>
> .   .   .   .   .

RICHARD   Then by myself—
ELIZABETH   Thy self is self-misused.
RICHARD   Now by the world—
ELIZABETH   'Tis full of thy foul
wrongs.
RICHARD   My father's death—
ELIZABETH   Thy life that hath
dishonoured.
RICHARD   Why then, by God—
ELIZABETH   God's wrong is most of
all.
    .   .   .   .   .
What canst thou swear by now?
RICHARD   The time to come.
ELIZABETH   That thou hast wrongèd in the time o'erpast.

                                        (4. 4. 297–319)

The rhythm of thrust-and-parry suggests, not improvisation, but
retribution: for every claim an answer, and a future already determined
by a history of unforgotten wrongs. As Richard's treacheries increasingly return to haunt him, the opposition to his wild singularity
becomes a massed chorus of voices, the audible counterpart to a world
of design which contains and finally destroys the anarchic Richard.

In *Romeo and Juliet* the conflict between improvisatory individual
wills and constraining design is carried in the metaphor of the stars.
The idea that our futures or fates are controlled by astrological pre-
determination is pooh-poohed in a later tragedy by the bastard,
Edmond: 'This is the excellent foppery of the world: that when we
are sick in fortune—often the surfeits of our own behaviour—we make
guilty of our disasters the sun, the moon, and stars . . . An admirable
evasion of whoremaster man, to lay his goatish disposition on the
charge of a star!' (*King Lear*, F, 1. 2. 116–26). In *Romeo and Juliet* the idea
is given sufficient dramatic weight to produce a sense of inevitability
out of the many accidents that lead to the lovers' deaths—and to show
that what we mean by tragic 'inevitability' is precisely not inevitable,
but the effect of technical contrivance, the artful arrangement of a plot.
The foreshadowing of doom is heavy throughout the play: Romeo has
not yet seen Juliet when already his 'mind misgives | Some con-
sequence yet hanging in the stars' which will 'expire the term | Of a

despisèd life' (1. 4. 106–10). Yet Juliet and Romeo nonetheless seem to us anything but helpless characters moved inexorably by powers beyond their control. The heady joy they take in their discovery of one another, the vibrancy of their passion, give to their play a thrilling sense of individual possibility, of limits, whether astrological or familial, overcome by the sheer force of their desire.

Juliet's efforts to affect the movement of time itself, to hurry it or slow it or stop it at the perfect moment of consummation, may remind us of Marlowe's Faustus in his final moments, desperately bidding the 'ever-moving spheres of heaven' to stand still (5. 2. 133). But Faustus knows that nothing will alter time's progress and that he has 'but one bare hour to live, | And then thou must be damned perpetually' (5. 2. 131–2). Juliet, by contrast, makes the Marlovian language a vehicle for an athletic eroticism which refuses to acknowledge limit:

> Gallop apace, you fiery-footed steeds,
> Towards Phoebus' lodging . . .
>
>   .   .   .   .   .
>
>   and Romeo
> Leap to these arms untalked of and unseen.
>
>   .   .   .   .   .
>
> Come night, come Romeo; come, thou day in night.
>   (3. 2. 1–2, 6–7, 17)

The play is filled with the idea of physical and emotional aspiration—leaping over garden walls, climbing up buildings, flying across distances. Anything seems possible to these young lovers. (Their very youthfulness, which would make them at home in comedy, makes them anomalous in Shakespeare's tragedies.) And the play takes its special kind of poignant beauty from the audience's knowledge that all their bursting energy of undulled sexual love will be foiled (and lamented) by a world as punishingly regular as the ever-moving stars.

In *Romeo and Juliet*, probably the second written of the plays listed in the Folio as a tragedy, Shakespeare most clearly experiments with the reciprocal relationship of the two chief kinds. The plot—two young lovers defy the barrier of parental edict to seek fulfilment in a world of their own making—might have been the plot of a comedy. Such a plot forms one of the strands of *A Midsummer Night's Dream* (written at about the same time as *Romeo and Juliet*), and it becomes, within that comedy, the basis for the plot of the hilariously botched play-within-the-play, the 'tedious brief scene' of 'Pyramus and Thisbe'. The lyrical language of *Romeo and Juliet*, with its sonnets, its aubade, its quick exchanges of wit, might also, with small variations, be the language of comedy. Even the heavily stressed sense that the lovers' future is fated despite their strong and hasty efforts to control it recalls comedy's way of moving its paired characters to the recognition of an ending which, despite the reluctance of the destined bride or groom, could never (it seems) have been otherwise. 'Never was a story of more woe | Than this of Juliet and her Romeo', says the Prince at the end; that sense of almost-sentimentalized 'woe' is all the greater because the comic possibilities are so close to the surface, the potential for a comic resolution so tantalizingly near.

It's a long way from hot, quick, passionate Verona to the darkness of *Macbeth*'s Scotland. But *Macbeth* raises questions about the illusion of characters' improvisatory freedom versus the already shaped destiny of their plot in an especially demanding way. Those questions involve further questions about the tragic character's moral status, about the degree of his or her self-awareness, and about the audience's response to the character and the play. If Macbeth has always been fated to kill Duncan (and that is one way of taking the three witches' equivocal prophecy), then Macbeth is indeed, to borrow Edmond's sarcastic phrase from *King Lear*, a villain 'on necessity'. Yet no character in Shakespeare considers his options with as much apparent lucidity as Macbeth. What he does, he does in full knowledge of what he himself calls the 'consequence'. Two prophecies have come true; like a more plodding but also more tortured Richard III, Macbeth records his response:

> Two truths are told
> As happy prologues to the swelling act
> Of the imperial theme. . . .
> This supernatural soliciting
> Cannot be ill, cannot be good. If ill,
> Why hath it given me earnest of success
> Commencing in a truth? I am Thane of Cawdor.
> If good, why do I yield to that suggestion
> Whose horrid image doth unfix my hair
> And make my seated heart knock at my ribs

Against the use of nature? Present fears
Are less than horrible imaginings.
My thought, whose murder yet is but fantastical,
Shakes so my single state of man that function
Is smothered in surmise, and nothing is
But what is not.

(1. 3. 126–41)

Here, at its best, is the Shakespearian way of creating characters who seem to create themselves by imitating the sound of a mind literally making itself up. The sickening back-and-forth rhythms ('cannot be ill, cannot be good'), the imagery of the self at war with itself ('my seated heart knock at my ribs', 'Shakes so my single state of man'), the sound of a mind puzzling over its inability fully to know itself ('why do I yield') give us the impression of a *person*, not a pawn. Can all this intense scrutiny of the bases for his actions be irrelevant in light of the witches' knowledge that, whatever Macbeth thinks, he has no choice but to fulfil their prophecy? We notice in this soliloquy that Macbeth is shaken by his own 'imaginings', by a 'murder' in (or is it *of*?) his 'thought'. The witches tell Macbeth that he will be king; they don't tell him how. Macbeth imagines the murder which will make him king— an imagining which seems to spring from himself and, in the same moment, to torment him with knowledge of his own unavoidable destruction.

In Milton's *Paradise Lost* the fallen angels divide into affinity groups to pass away eternity. Some go in for athletics, others for war-games. 'Others apart sat on a hill retired, | In thoughts more elevate, and reasoned high | Of providence, foreknowledge, will, and fate, | Fixed fate, free will, foreknowledge absolute, | And found no end, in wandering mazes lost' (Book II, 567–71). That hellish seminar may warn us against trying to solve the puzzle of foreknowledge (of the three witches' sort) and free will (of the sort that Macbeth may, or may not, possess). In *Macbeth*, Shakespeare does not attempt to solve but to use this conundrum of Christian theology for specifically theatrical effect. Lady Macbeth's immediate reaction to the prophecy is to try to occupy, immediately, the promised future, as if the consequential movement of tomorrow and tomorrow and tomorrow could somehow be finessed: 'Thy letters have transported me beyond | This ignorant present, and I feel now | The future in the instant' (1. 5. 55–7). Macbeth's

own further reaction ('If it were done when 'tis done, then 'twere well |
It were done quickly' (1. 7. 1–2)) is remarkable because it so clearly spells
out all the reasons why it will *not* be well to kill Duncan. Macbeth
knows that the assassination cannot 'trammel up the consequence':
killing Duncan will not be 'the be-all and the end-all'. There will be
judgement in the hereafter; but even if he were to risk eternal damnation still there will be bad consequences in the here-and-now. Murder-
ing Duncan will, he knows, 'teach | Bloody instructions' so that the
deed will return and 'plague th'inventor'. He knows that he will have to
drink from his own 'poisoned chalice'. He knows that the laws of
kinship and hospitality speak loudly against his deed. He knows that
Duncan has been so 'meek' and 'clear in his great office, that his virtues
| Will plead like angels, trumpet-tongued against | The deep damna-
tion of his taking-off' (1.7.18–20). Finally he conjures for himself the
apocalyptic image of 'pity, like a naked new-born babe, | Striding the
blast' (21–2), and of the tears shed for Duncan's murder 'drown[ing] the
wind'. Macbeth has no spur to prick him on to do the deed; the best he
can find as a positive against the long and powerful list of negatives is a
word, 'ambition', which begs more questions than it answers.

Why then does Macbeth persist in a course of action he knows is
both morally wrong and practically doomed? Why does he go on
butchering enemies long after it becomes apparent that the future
will not be his? There will be no Macbeth dynasty: 'unlineal hands'
will grasp the crown, while Macbeth and Lady Macbeth, dead without
heirs, will lead fools the way to dusty death. The spectacle of Macbeth
and Lady Macbeth murdering their own humanity in the process of
murdering others gives the tragedy its distinctive sense of claustropho-
bic madness, of suicidal determination. Macbeth is a tyrant, yet we do
not react to him with loathing. Lady Macbeth, who would dash out her
baby's brains to accomplish her purpose, thinks that a little water will
clear them of the deed, yet the spectacle of her madness and suicide
gives the audience no great sense of satisfaction. Macbeth and Lady
Macbeth suffer the consequences of their actions; they know themselves remorselessly. The response to their tragedy is not an easy sense
of justice served. The Aristotelian pair of tragic emotions, 'pity and
fear', points towards the more complex response the play elicits.

So does the pair Horatio uses to characterize another tragic story:
'What is it ye would see? | If aught of *woe or wonder*, cease your search'

(*Hamlet*, 5. 2. 316–17, italics added). In *Hamlet*, too, a supernatural voice, the imperious voice of the ghostly father commanding his son to 'Revenge his foul and most unnatural murder' (1. 5. 25), seems to summon Hamlet to his destiny. Yet Hamlet questions that destiny almost as tenaciously as he embraces it; and his sweeping to it 'with wings as swift | As meditation or the thoughts of love' (1. 5. 29–30) is blocked by the 'pale cast' of other thoughts. Hamlet's 'conscience' may make a coward of his resolution to enact a swift revenge, but it also makes him the hero of thought—of intense self-consciousness—itself. Convention and literary history—in a word, genre—also summon him to his destiny. Shakespeare's Hamlet is reworked from the Hamlet of an earlier (lost) play, probably by Thomas Kyd. Kyd's vastly popular *The Spanish Tragedy* had, as we saw in Chapter 2, begun the fashion for an English form of Senecan tragedy with a revenger as its morally ambiguous hero; and Hieronimo's mad deviousness, his rhetorical excess, even his desperate use of play-acting within the play established audience-expectations which it is Hamlet's theatrical destiny to fulfil. But with differences, of course, for *Hamlet*, like Hamlet, seems determined at times *not* to fulfil the expectations of its kind. Kyd's Elizabethan play is set in Spain; Jacobean plays which partake of revenge as a motor for dramatic action are sometimes set in Italy: in those hot and hot-tempered Catholic countries, the deviousness (moral and dramaturgic) of the revenge-plot is apparently meant to seem natural. *Hamlet*, of course, is set in icy Denmark. In other, more significant ways too, it shows Shakespeare questioning a genre's conventions in the process of using them.

The idea of revenge gives a sense of virtually ritualized mission to character and plot. A task is proposed: it has the trappings of a religious duty, a calling, which is not diminished but strangely enhanced by the moral dubiousness of that mission. (Kyd's Hieronimo quotes God's words, '*Vindicta mihi*': vengeance is *mine* [not man's], *I* will repay; and he immediately misappropriates those words to justify his assumption of the divine prerogative.) But a sense of mission informs more tragedies than those which fall under the rubric of 'revenge tragedies'. One critic speaks helpfully of 'revenge as the metaphor for action' (that is, the necessity of 'action' is primary, and 'revenge' is the form of action that can symbolize that necessity); it is a metaphor which 'produced an extreme vision, one of almost unprecedented darkness'.[4] The darkness of that 'extreme vision' is peculiarly English and, to an extent, Shakespearian. (The greatest Greek version of a 'revenge tragedy', Aeschylus's *Oresteia* trilogy, ends with a vote to end the cycle of revenge and to inaugurate an order of non-retributive justice.) One curious fact about 'revenge as the metaphor for action' is that, in the Jacobean plays that followed *Hamlet*, and which clearly owe much to it, it is often hard to know who is revenging himself on whom for what. Revenge becomes, in a sense, not only a metaphor for action but for action muddled, contradictory, incapable of straightforward resolution. At the beginning of John Webster's *The White Devil* (1612), Lodovico opens the play with the one grim word, 'Banished!' And indeed he spends much of the play off-stage, while 'the white devil', Vittoria, and her brother, Flamineo, take centre stage. It may therefore come as a surprise, to an audience struggling to follow the complex plot, that after Vittoria's and Flamineo's eloquently drawn-out deaths, the banished Lodovico announces (as he's about to be taken off for torture and execution) that *he* 'limned this night piece' and intends to 'call this act [his] own'. But it is a real question, in that play and others, who, if anyone, can claim final agency for an action ('revenge') which seems to spin out of control and become not a specific deed but a general condition. The revenger tries to take control of the plot and drive it to a conclusion in the one death that will crown his mission. But that one death becomes many, and the revenger's own death is inevitably among them.

In this light, many of Shakespeare's tragedies can be thought of in an extended sense as 'revenge tragedies'. Othello, once he is under Iago's sway, thinks he is an actor in a play far different from the one we see. In his play, Desdemona is 'that cunning whore of Venice | That married with Othello' (4. 2. 93–4). And in the play created by his sick imagining, Othello takes up revenge as a moral duty. He can leave Cassio's death to Iago, but with Desdemona he imposes upon himself the role of judge and executioner: 'It is the cause, it is the cause, my soul. | Let me not name it to you, you chaste stars. It is the cause' (5. 2. 1–3). So he enters the bedroom where Desdemona sleeps upon their wedding sheets, convinced that 'she must die, else she'll betray more men'. In the very bizarreness of his justification—he will execute Desdemona not on his own behalf but in order to protect all those other men she would otherwise betray—we hear the revenger's sense of mission. And like other revengers, Othello acts in sorrow as well as anger, convinced that he is doing heaven's work: 'I must weep, | But they are cruel tears. This sorrow's heavenly, | It strikes where it doth love' (5. 2. 20–3). In *Othello* revenge is both the compelling metaphor for action and a fatally grotesque mistake. At the end of *Hamlet*, Horatio summarizes the plot as one 'Of carnal, bloody, and unnatural acts, | Of accidental judgements, casual slaughters, | Of deaths put on by cunning and forced cause; | And, in this upshot, purposes mistook | Fall'n on th'inventors' heads' (5. 2. 335–9). Othello's determination to become the justified hero of a revenge tragedy leads him into a similar mad web of crossed-purposes and deadly mistake.

Brutus, in *Julius Caesar*, is, like Othello, determined that his action will not be a murder but a justified, even a religious, sacrifice. His commitment to the conspiracy comes only after he has agonizingly overcome his scruples, but it immediately leads to the extreme conclusion, 'It must be by his death' (2. 1. 10). Not any kind of death, and certainly not murder: 'Let's be sacrificers, but not butchers, Caius' (2. 1. 166). Brutus is not deluded in the way Othello is, yet his action too may be as much a mistake as it is a righteous mission. In *Julius Caesar*, mistake and mission are hard to separate because both the political issues and the characters' motives—those of Caesar and Antony, on the one hand, and Brutus, Cassius, and the conspirators, on the other—repel the reductiveness of moralistic judgements: one person's 'noblest Roman of them all' is a 'savage' in the judgement of another. And the play itself enacts our critical debates. So Antony, as if directly answering Brutus's claim to be a sacrificer but not a butcher, addresses the dead Caesar: 'O pardon me, thou bleeding piece of earth, | That I am meek and gentle with these *butchers*' (3. 1. 257–8; italics added). The play enacts our critical divisions in another way as well, for in this odd version of revenge tragedy there is more than one mission and more than one revenge. The play's structure has often seemed a puzzle. In the first half, we attend especially to the sacrifice of Caesar. But the second half is Caesar's posthumous revenge. Brutus, the sacrificer or murderer of the play's early scenes, becomes the hunted victim, the sacrifice, of the later scenes, pursued by the spirit of Caesar. And it is a role he accepts, as other of Shakespeare's tragic heroes, including Hamlet, accept their own death as the fitting end of the plot: 'I shall have glory by this losing day. . . . My bones would rest, | That have but laboured to attain this hour' (5. 5. 36, 41–2).

So revenge in Shakespearian tragedy is not the property only of a special sub-class of plays but one of the motives, often mixed or thwarted or perverted from its intention, which impart a sense of dramatic inevitability to the action. King Lear, in the impotent rage of his impending madness, warns his daughters,

> I will have such revenges on you both
> That all the world shall—I will do such things—
> What they are, yet I know not; but they shall be
> The terrors of the earth.
>
> (F, 2. 2. 453–6)

His 'revenges' will make the world . . . what? Sit up and take notice? Recognize that a necesssary action has reached its destined conclusion? He cannot say. And he cannot say what things he will do. But he knows that they must terrify the earth itself. What he cannot know is that the consummating action will not be the punishment of Goneril and Regan. When the sisters' dead bodies are brought forth, Albany pronounces that 'This judgement of the heavens, that makes us tremble, | Touches us not with pity' (F, 5. 3. 206–7): the spectacle makes us fearful of God's judgement but, because it is a just judgement, it does not inspire the other tragic emotion, pity. Lear's own death and, more than that, Cordelia's death, are the actions towards which the play drives.

Yet it might have been otherwise: Cordelia's death is not required by the sources Shakespeare drew on for *King Lear*, in which Cordelia dies many years after Lear. It is not required by generic expectation, which could be satisfied with the play's heap of deaths—Cornwall's, Gloucester's, Goneril's, Regan's, Lear's—without the almost superfluous cruelty of Cordelia's death. And it was, apparently, not required by subsequent theatre history. In 1681 the playwright Nahum Tate 'improved' *King Lear* by rewriting it to accommodate the sensibilities of a later generation of theatre-goers. For his more neo-classically inclined audience he removed the character of the Fool, so that majestical matters would not be infected with the actions of clowns. And he noticed that Shakespeare had almost perversely missed a fine theatrical opportunity: he had provided the play with two virtuous and eligible young people, Cordelia and Edgar, but had never once allowed them to appear together on stage until Cordelia is dead. Tate improved matters by creating a love interest between the two; and his play ends, not with Cordelia's death, but with her marriage to Edgar, while Lear (also alive) opts for retirement to a life of contemplation.

Tate's 'improved' *King Lear* is more than a bizarre footnote to theatrical history: his happy ending was the only one performed on English stages for the next 150 years. Its success shows that generic conventions are historically determined rather than universal. For Tate and later eighteenth-century audiences, Shakespeare's conception of tragedy seemed a mistake caused by his imperfect understanding of the 'rules' of generic decorum. And that mistake was not simply aesthetic but moral as well. No less a critic than Samuel Johnson defended Tate's version against Shakespeare's own. The death of Cordelia offended Johnson's sense of how plays should work because it offended his Christian sense of how the world, under God's providence, should work: 'Shakespeare has suffered the virtue of Cordelia to perish in a just cause, contrary to the natural ideas of justice'. Johnson knows that real life is full of injustice; but the artist's obligation is not to imitate the world's imperfect justice but instead a 'poetical justice' which represents the sometimes hard to discern goodness of God: 'A play in which the wicked prosper and the virtuous miscarry may doubtless be good, because it is a just [accurate] representation of the common events of human life; but since all reasonable beings naturally love justice, I cannot easily be persuaded that the observation of justice makes a play worse; or that, if other excellencies are equal, the audience will not always rise better pleased from the final triumph of persecuted virtue.'[5] It is all too easy for us today to laugh at Johnson's passionate commitment to an unconditional, inborn 'justice' that all 'reasonable beings' supposedly feel; his desire to see 'the final triumph of persecuted virtue' sounds sentimental or moralistic. But it is precisely because of his moral sense that Johnson can recognize the truly extraordinary thing that Shakespeare has done in *King Lear*. Johnson's personal testimony—'I was many years ago so shocked by Cordelia's death that I know not whether I ever endured to read again the last scenes of the play till I undertook to revise them as an editor'—records his undulled, unbearably painful response to the very real challenge Shakespeare's tragedy poses to any comforting belief about 'natural justice'.

A few years after *Lear*, in *The Tempest*, Shakespeare created another ageing man who feels himself the victim of familial ingratitude and dedicates himself to righting his wrongs. But Prospero, unlike the impotent Lear, is well able to carry out his plans. *The Tempest* is a romance or tragicomedy, but what happens in it is one of the possibilities inherent in the use of revenge as 'the metaphor for action'. Will Prospero, now that he has his enemies at his command, use his powers for revenge? There isn't very much suspense about this: the play's generic intentions are bound up with Prospero's dynastic intention to marry his daughter to the son of the King of Naples. Miranda pities the victims of Prospero's magical storm, but he assures her that 'I have done nothing but in care of thee, | Of thee, my dear one, thee my daughter' (1. 2. 16–17). *The Tempest*, like the other late romances, shows Shakespeare playing flexibly with generic expectation and recognizing that tragedy and comedy depend on one another. The tragic potential is contained within the comic design of exile, recognition, and homecoming. Prospero plays the heavy father, the *senex* who erects barriers to young love: the story of Miranda and Ferdinand could be a story like that of *Romeo and Juliet*. Yet Prospero keeps the lovers apart only so that he can, on his own terms, remove the barriers he erects: he licenses the sexual desire of Miranda and Ferdinand by making that desire, in marriage, the way to fulfil his purpose. And he turns away from the design of revenge to the design of reconciliation. Ariel's tender response to the spectacle of old Gonzalo's sorrow reminds Prospero that he is 'one of their kind'. Although struck to the quick by their wrongs, he decides that 'The rarer action is | In virtue than in vengeance' (5. 1. 27–8). Certainly it is the rarer action in tragedy. The motifs of *The Tempest* turn out to be comic motifs—the dispersal of a family, the wandering across dangerous seas to a strange place of potential transformation, homecoming and marriage—but they contain within themselves the stuff of tragedy, not least in Prospero's strong need for the vengeance he finally abjures.

Expressing the Inexpressible

The Tempest comes at the end of Shakespeare's exploration into the uses of revenge as a motor for tragic action. *Titus Andronicus* comes at the start. It was his first tragedy, but separated by only six or seven years from *Hamlet*. It is tempting for a modern audience to feel superior to this play of extreme rhetoric and extreme situations. It does contain one of Shakespeare's worst half-lines of verse, the announcement that 'Alarbus' limbs are lopped' (1. 1. 143). And Alarbus' aren't the only limbs that fall in the gruesome spectacle of mangled, diminished, suffering human beings. The patriarch Titus cuts off his hand; Queen Tamora is made to eat her murderous sons baked in a pie. The stage direction 'Enter... Lavinia, her hands cut off, her tongue cut out, and ravished' (2. 4) soundlessly says it all. But that is part of Shakespeare's point in this first, daring experiment in tragedy. Grotesquely deprived of the means to speak or write, the violated Lavinia still must make her meaning known. In the silent pain of extreme suffering she must find a way to represent herself to an unresponsive world. *Titus Andronicus* is a nightmare world of the unutterable scream, the unattainable release from horror through outcry or gesture. It shares that nightmare with its predecessor, Kyd's *The Spanish Tragedy*. Hieronimo cannot achieve satisfaction for his son's death through the use of words. As if to emblematize both the need for and the impossibility of language to assuage great grief, Hieronimo stages a play-within-the-play 'in sundry languages'; the actors (who die in earnest) include the murderers of his son. The incomprehensible Babel of the play-within-the-play represents the failure of Hieronimo's rhetoric to bring him the justice he requires. In his final gestures, Hieronimo bites out his tongue and then kills himself with the knife that is supposed to sharpen his pen. Language fails Hieronimo (but not Kyd), and Hieronimo in his final moments chooses death as the only appropriate action. In *Titus Andronicus* too, the play's elaborate, even excessive 'Senecan' rhetoric does not undo but underlines the paradox, that all the eloquent words in the world may still leave us speechless in the face of such horror.

Lavinia and her father Titus (handless and insane, his words deranged by the very pressure of his need for expression) share with other Shakespearian tragic figures a self-expressive task: as they suffer greatly and cause great suffering, they must speak greatly, their eloquence matching the pain. Titus is engaged in a definitively Shakespearian tragic action (despite the grotesquerie of the situation) when he swears to his speechless daughter

> Thou shalt not sigh, not hold thy stumps to heaven,
> Nor wink, nor nod, nor kneel, nor make a sign,
> But I of these will wrest an alphabet,
> And by still practice learn to know thy meaning.
>
> (3. 2. 42–5)

To 'wrest an alphabet' from the human form in agony and to find a language that will suffice is a central task for Shakespeare and his characters. But everywhere, although not as obviously as in *Titus*, the great difficulty of the task is apparent.

Hamlet claims that all his expressive means—his mourning clothes, his sighs and gestures—cannot 'denote him truly'; yet he tries repeatedly to externalize 'that within which passes show', only to find that he has inadequately 'unpack[ed] his heart with words'. The play is full of communicative tangles, when Hamlet fails (or refuses) to make himself understood by the other characters or, really, by the audience. The mad-speech Hamlet feigns becomes Ophelia's speech in earnest, as though only a crazed language can express the madness of a world where her lover and father figuratively tear her apart, as Lavinia is literally torn in *Titus Andronicus*. *King Lear*, the play which most nearly matches *Titus* in sheer physical horrors, begins with a ritual, the love-trial, which demands that its participants speak but which silences all who refuse to stay within its restrictive rules. On the heath, in the storm, the discordant dialogue of a fool, a crazy king, and a bedlam beggar becomes the play's best language, which discovers what the courtly language hid.

Othello begins his stage career confident that he can be fully known, that others will recognize him as, he believes, he essentially is: 'My parts, my title, and my perfect soul | Shall manifest me rightly' (1. 2. 31–2); but the ensuing action mocks his confidence in the unequivocal adequacy of his self-representation. Condemned by Desdemona's father, Othello stands before the Venetian Senate and proudly delivers 'a round unvarnished tale' of his whole course of love. Othello's words convince the Duke ('I think this tale would win my daughter, too' (1. 3. 170)), but they become, in only slightly revised form, the words of Iago's counter-story about an 'erring barbarian' and a 'super-subtle Venetian'. Iago tells Othello a subtly revised version of Othello's own 'tale'—'She did deceive her father, marrying you | And when she seemed to shake and fear your looks | She loved them most. . . . Why, go to, then. | She that so young could give out such a seeming' (3. 3. 210–13)—and unleashes the social and psychic disruptiveness latent in it. The play discovers a dangerous gap between Othello's confident assertion of stable self-presence—of a 'perfect soul' perfectly expressed by its outward signs and symbols—and the slippery misrepresentations, intentional or not, of language itself. Othello's final directions, to the audiences on stage and off, 'Speak of me as I am. Nothing extenuate, | Nor set down aught in malice' (5. 2. 351–2), seem nearly impossible to fulfil in light of that revealed elusiveness. To speak of Othello as he is, without special pleading on either side, would require nothing less than the re-enactment of the play itself: no reductive judgement drawn from it can encompass the complexity of a character who, in his dying gesture, identifies himself simultaneously as his society's saving hero and its most dangerous enemy:

> Say... that in Aleppo once,
> Where a malignant and a turbaned Turk
> Beat a Venetian and traduced the state,
> I took by th' throat the circumcisèd dog
> And smote him thus.
> *He stabs himself.*
>
> (5. 2. 361–5)

Othello's dying wish to have us speak the truth about him echoes Hamlet's. With virtually his last words, Hamlet demands that Horatio absent himself from the felicity of death 'And in this harsh world draw thy breath in pain | To tell my story' (5. 2. 300–1). But Horatio's memorial task has already been fulfilled in the only way it can be; as Northrop Frye writes, 'At the end of *Hamlet* we get a strong feeling that the play we are watching is, in a sense, Horatio's story.'[6]

In two late tragedies Shakespeare rings his most surprising changes on the tragic character's expressive task. Coriolanus virtually refuses to speak. He will not ask the plebeians for their votes (or 'voices'); he will not show them the scars of battle which should speak for him. His aim is to express himself solely through his deeds in the moment of their doing; he tries to avoid that dangerous space Othello discovers between words and things. He is the least soliloquizing of Shakespeare's tragic characters; his most poignantly expressive moment is, literally, wordless: as his mother pleads that he not destroy his own city of Rome the stage direction reads, '*He holds her by the hand, silent*' (5. 3. *s.d.* 183). That silence is Coriolanus's most characteristic expression. In production it should be held as long as possible. But finally Coriolanus must speak, because he is, despite his best efforts, human. He satisfies his mother, and in the process of trying to reintegrate himself with the society of his birth is literally torn apart by his new allies. 'Tear him to pieces!' is the cry of the many against this resolute one whose proudest claim is 'Alone I did it' (5. 6. 121, 117).

But in his other late Roman play Shakespeare created, in Cleopatra, his most exuberantly self-expressive, self-creative tragic character. Two truths are told in *Antony and Cleopatra*; the play gives each its contradictory due. One is the sordid truth seen through the unillusioned eyes of the literal-minded Romans, in which Cleopatra is a middle-aged whore who uses her seductiveness for personal power and entraps the generous but foolish Antony to his doom. The other is the imaginative truth created by Cleopatra and Antony. They not only tell, they become their own lavish myth. Cleopatra re-creates herself as the very spirit of the Nile valley's lush fertility; her language makes her not an ageing sex-object but the beloved partner of the sun-god himself: 'Think on me, | That am with Phoebus' amorous pinches black | And wrinkled deep in time' (1. 5. 27–9). In this version of the play's truth, her fickleness becomes an 'infinite variety', the overflowing abundance of the Nile itself. Antony's improvidence becomes, in Cleopatra's mythic version, a kind of cosmic generosity:

> For his bounty,
> There was no winter in't; an autumn 'twas,
> That grew the more by reaping. His delights
> Were dolphin-like; they showed his back above
> The element they lived in. In his livery
> Walked crowns and crownets. Realms and islands were
> As plates dropped from his pocket.
>
> (5. 2. 85–91)

In the world of Cleopatra's rich imagination death itself is sexualized and made the goal of ecstatic consummation. A tragedy that ends in death also ends, by Cleopatra's imaginative fiat, with a triumphal marriage:

Give me my robe. Put on my crown. I have
Immortal longings in me....

> .   .   .   .

Husband, I come.
Now to that name my courage prove my title.

> .   .   .   .

The stroke of death is as a lover's pinch,
Which hurts and is desired....

> .   .   .   .

O Antony!

(5. 2. 275–307)

Cleopatra tells her own story. It is not the only story the play tells. But it has, against all Roman evidence to the contrary, its own compelling truth. The Folio designates that story a tragedy, as it should, but in Cleopatra's version it is a tragedy with a happy ending.

Gender and Genre: What Do (Tragic) Men Want?

Cleopatra's expressive self-creativity is unusual not only in degree; among the tragedies it is absolutely unusual because she is a woman. It is not entirely accurate, as I pointed out in a previous chapter, to say that tragedy is the masculine genre, comedy the feminine genre. The 'happy ending' of Shakespearian comedy took place within a social order where a wife, by scriptural and legal warrant, was supposed to submit to the headship of her husband. (Yet that social order, from 1558 through 1603, was ruled by Queen Elizabeth.) Members of a modern audience may object that the comic resolution serves to secure that social order at women's expense. Women may be rendered literally speechless in comedies. Isabella has no scripted response to the Duke's marriage proposal at the end of *Measure for Measure*. But that is one of the things that make *Measure for Measure* a so-called problem play; our uncertain response to the end of *Measure for Measure* suggests that the silencing of woman is an action more appropriate on the tragic than the comic stage.

The mutilated Lavinia, in *Titus Andronicus*, is the initial emblem of woman's tragic silencing. The irrepressible Juliet, like Cleopatra, is exceptional; but in the roughly contemporaneous *Julius Caesar* Portia is a scarcely-present figure, sequestered from the political action which

Brutus identifies as entirely men's work. Desdemona's death by stran-
gulation literalizes Othello's failure to hear her plain words of love,
deafened as he is by the masculine madness of possessive jealousy.
Ophelia, torn between lover and father, a pawn in the deadly male
game of revenge, is driven to the desperate expressive expedient of
madness and suicide. Lady Macbeth, by contrast with the relatively
passive, victimized Ophelia, is a whirlwind of aggressive energy. For
that very reason she becomes identified, not as male but (like the three
witches) as something not-quite-female: she invokes the powers that
tend on mortal thoughts to 'Unsex me here'; she would exchange the
milk of her female body for gall, and conversely she fears that her
hesitant husband is 'too full o' th' milk of human kindness' (1. 5. 16). But
after Duncan's murder she is increasingly marginal to the action;
Macbeth keeps her 'ignorant of the knowledge' of his further murders.
Macbeth wades through rivers of blood ('I am in blood | Stepped in so
far that, should I wade no more, | Returning were as tedious as go o'er'
(3. 4. 135– 7)), while she compulsively tries to wash away the bloody
stain of guilt. In the play, madness and suicide figure as the return of
her repressed femininity, her fate for having denied the normative
masculine definition of the womanly.

　None of this convicts Shakespeare, or even Shakespearian tragedy, of
misogyny. Female victimization is dramatized in the tragedies, and later
in the romances, as precisely that: victimization. Only Lady Macbeth
and, in a very different way, Cleopatra, can even crudely be said to
deserve their fates. And the male habit of blaming women, however
frequently it occurs, is marked as pathological, a disease rather than a
right of man. The disease is painful, even destructive, for victimizer as
well as victim. Lear is crazy—and everyone on stage knows he is crazy—
when he wilfully refuses to hear Cordelia: 'Nothing will come of
nothing. Speak again.' What he will not hear in Act 1 he desperately
tries to hear in Act 5, when it is too late: 'Her voice was ever soft, |
Gentle, and low, an excellent thing in woman' (F, 5. 3. 247–8). In between
comes the old king's vast rage, provoked by his new awareness of social
injustice but also by his fearfully anxious imagining of female sexuality:

> Down from the waist
> They're centaurs, though women all above.
> But to the girdle do the gods inherit;

> Beneath is all the fiend's. There's hell, there's darkness,
> there is the sulphurous pit, burning, scalding, stench,
> consumption. Fie, fie fie; pah, pah! Give me an ounce of
> civet, good apothecary, sweeten my imagination.
>
> (F, 4. 5. 121–7)

Lear's reunion with Cordelia is figured not only as the cure for this madness ('O my dear father, restoration hang | Thy medicine on my lips' (F, 4. 6. 23–4)) but also as a kind of birth after death ('You do me wrong to take me out o' th'grave' F, 4.6.38)). His anxious rage against the threat of female sexuality is one pole of Lear's tragedy; his reciprocal, abject need for female nurture is the other.

The tragic man's fear of female sexuality is also his fear of woman's freedom from masculine control. In *Othello*, *The Winter's Tale*, and *Cymbeline* no one but the jealous husband believes that his wife has been unfaithful. But the jealous husbands cannot *believe* what they think they cannot *know*.[7] They demand a kind of evidential certainty, a controlling absoluteness of knowledge, which is impossible when the object of knowledge is another human being. Othello desperately requires that Iago prove his love a whore: 'Give me the ocular proof. . . . Make me to see't' (3. 3. 365, 369): the uncertainty of human otherness is more terrifying to him than the (supposed) certainty of knowing the worst. For Othello it is the 'curse of marriage, | That we can call these delicate creatures ours | And not their appetites' (3. 3. 272–4). What cannot be seen—the thoughts, the feelings, the 'appetites' of another person—cannot be possessed; and if not possessed, 'these delicate creatures' cannot be what Othello, in masculine solidarity, calls 'ours'. In *The Winter's Tale*, Leontes, like Othello, is most mad when most convinced of his rightness. He turns his fear of female unpossessibility into a universal condition, one shared, in his grotesque conceit, with the men in the audience to his own play:

> And many a man there is, even at this present,
> Now, while I speak this, holds his wife by th' arm,
> That little thinks she has been sluiced in's absence,
> And his pond fished by his next neighbour, by
> Sir Smile, his neighbour.
>
> (1. 2. 193–7)

Leontes constructs an idea of the female body as fluid, uncontainable. Or as a sexualized city under siege, where a treacherous population embraces the invader:

> From east, west, north, and south, be it concluded:
> No barricado for a belly. Know't,
> It will let in and out the enemy
> With bag and baggage.
>
> (1. 2. 204–7)

The jealous husband misrecognizes his own fearful fantasy as a triumph of reason and knowledge. Othello takes the handkerchief as proof, and on that crazy presumption of objective certainty he commits himself to Iago's fantasy-world. Leontes constructs an elaborate conceit to describe his acquisition of a 'knowledge' that the play recognizes as sickness:

> There may be in the cup
> A spider steeped, and one may drink, depart,
> And yet partake no venom, for his knowledge
> Is not infected; but if one present
> Th'abhorred ingredient to his eye, make known
> How he hath drunk, he cracks his gorge, his sides,
> With violent hefts. I have drunk, and seen the spider.
>
> (2. 1. 41–7)

Leontes's 'knowledge' is the symptom of his disease, the incapacity to believe what he fears he cannot know. Leontes and his kingdom will live a kind of life-in-death, without an heir, until that which is lost is found. The recovery of the lost one, Perdita, is the long-awaited event which can restore Leontes to his own future. But in this romance even more is granted. 'It is required', says Paulina, showing the statue of Hermione, 'You do awake your faith' (5. 3. 94–5). The exiled female returns in the form of Hermione's living likeness, the animated work of art.

Masculine anxiety about female sexual self-possession is one symptom of the tragic protagonist's more general desire for knowledge, for control, for a kind of power over a world which, like a wife, cannot be ruled in the way the absolutist demands. Shakespeare's tragic protagonists make great demands upon their worlds, and eventually those worlds refuse to sustain the demand. Hamlet, that most intellectually searching of tragic heroes, with his ultimate questions about being and nothingness, also questions, with an uncontrolled anger comparable to Othello's or Leontes', the 'honesty' of both Gertrude and Ophelia. Hamlet's quest throughout the play is in certain ways excessive. The ghost tells him about the murder: but was it *really* his father's ghost? The play-within-the-play proves it was an honest ghost: but now how should Hamlet act? Ophelia thinks he loved her once: she should not have believed him, he says, with the anger of a disappointed lover. Leave your mother to heaven, the ghost commands: but Hamlet speaks daggers to her for living 'In the rank sweat of an enseamèd bed, | Stewed in corruption, honeying and making love | Over the nasty sty' (3. 4. 82–4). Sigmund Freud notoriously asked, 'What does a woman want?' For a moment I want to ask, 'What does a man want, when he is the protagonist of a Shakespearian tragedy?'

There is a clue in the very titles. We know the comedies by the names of their occasions or situations: *The Comedy of Errors, A Midsummer Night's Dream, Twelfth Night, As You Like It*. The rule isn't inviolable, though where it is broken—as in *The Merchant of Venice*—critics and audiences have suspected the presence of 'problems' or authorial mistakes. Conversely, we know the tragedies by the names of their remarkable individuals: Hamlet and *Hamlet*, Othello and *Othello*, King Lear and *King Lear*. In comedy, the individual tends to be subordinated to the actions of the whole; in tragedy, the whole is dominated by the actions of the remarkable individual. As in all matters having to do with genre, the distinction is far from absolute. Society is present in tragedy as it is in comedy. Coriolanus thinks there is a world elsewhere; despising the city, he turns his back to live where he thinks he is most comfortable, 'alone'. But the most a-social of tragic characters, like Coriolanus or Timon of Athens, discover that there is no escaping the social world. Timon in the wilderness digs the earth and in it finds the gold which he thinks has been the root of his problems within the social world. Coriolanus, by the play's relentless logic, finds himself not just out of Rome but in the city of Rome's enemy. He tries to deny his wife, child, friend, even his powerful mother; but he finds that to deny them is to deny himself—and to acknowledge them is to accede to his own destruction. The tragic protagonist is anything but a man alone; but his demand, nonetheless, is for a kind of singular identity which is also an imposition of his singular will upon the resistant world.

Othello's 'make me to see it', Lear's 'which of you shall we say doth love us most', Hamlet's search for 'that within which passes show' are instances of that imposition. From the comic point of view, Troilus is just another young fool in love; from the tragic side he is a man desperately searching for a solid foundation of certain truth in a dramatic universe which repels his demand for certainty. Troilus cannot accept the 'attest of eyes and ears' (5. 2. 124) which gives him evidence that Cressida is unfaithful. Her individual guilt may be less the problem than Troilus's unwillingness to accept that time changes circumstance, and that 'truth' may be contingent on time. If it was once thought good that the Trojans should fight to keep Helen, then they must go on fighting to keep Helen, no matter how many thousands of deaths it costs; if Cressida was once Troilus's Cressida she must always be Troilus's Cressida, for to acknowledge the possibility of change would force this absolutist to acknowledge his own mortal dependency on time. Macbeth learns two truths which seem to guarantee the third, that he will be king hereafter. But rather than submit to the reassuringly regular pace of tomorrow and tomorrow and tomorrow he tries to seize the promised future and violently wrench into the present what should have been hereafter. Lear, near the end of life, wants 'To shake all cares and business from our age' so that he can 'Unburdened crawl toward death' (F, 1. 1. 39, 41), but the love-trial he engineers is a power-play aimed against futurity itself. Dividing his kingdom is an act of self-dispossession, but it is also an effort to control his world by acquiring an impossible certainty. It is a holding on rather than a letting go.

At the end of the period in which he most intensively explored the possibilities of tragic form, Shakespeare returned, with differences, to the material of his earlier comedies—to shipwrecks, reunions, and reconciliation. In the late romances, especially *The Winter's Tale* and *The Tempest*, Shakespeare's impossibly demanding protagonists are given a kind of second chance: comedy finds them in the midst of their tragic quests. Prospero's island is potentially the site for either comic forgiveness or tragic revenge, and neither possibility is forgotten, even when the magician sets his 'nobler reason' against his 'fury' because 'The rarer action is | In virtue than in vengeance' (5. 1. 27–8).

'Full fathom five' in the sea that surrounds *The Tempest*'s stage-like island a body lies, at once decaying and being remade, its dead bones becoming living coral and its eyes changed to pearls. The death figured in Ariel's song is painful, yet there is beauty in it; it is an image of great loss and of great gain all at once.

The tragicomedy of *The Tempest* is the product of a specific moment in theatre history which favoured the mingling of genres. But the implications of the form, at least as Shakespeare practised it in his last romances, had been glimpsed a millennium earlier. At the end of Plato's *Symposium*, his account of a long night's talking about the nature of love and life, a band of revellers intrude on the fun, 'and everyone was compelled to drink large quantities of wine'. Some of the participants left, some fell asleep; one of them, Aristodemus, scarcely awake, vaguely recalled that Socrates stayed up drinking and talking with the comic poet Aristophanes and the tragedian Agathon. The wine, the hour, the mysteriousness of Socrates' words make the whole business dream-like, a truth barely glimpsed in passing: Aristodemus 'did not hear the beginning of the discourse; the chief thing which he remembered was Socrates compelling the other two to acknowledge that the genius of comedy was the same with that of tragedy, and that the true artist in tragedy was an artist in comedy also. To this they were constrained to assent, being drowsy, and not quite following the argument.'[8]

WHAT has become of the genres? I go to my video store and find a
whole section called Comedy. But none called Tragedy or Satire or
History or Tragicomedy. Instead there's a huge undifferentiated section called Drama. For tragedies I have to look in a small section called
Classics: mostly what I find there are Shakespeare's tragedies, mixed
up with some of his comedies and some BBC adaptations of Victorian
novels. There are a few tragedies by modern playwrights—Eugene
O'Neill's *Mourning Becomes Electra*, Tennessee Williams's *A Streetcar
Named Desire*, Arthur Miller's *Death of a Salesman*; but they strike me
as attempts to revive a category no one in the video store believes in any
more. Where did it go, the whole elaborate structure of genre-theory
and its related practice from Aristotle to Alexander Pope?

Two answers in conclusion. First, what my video store (that handy
microcosm of modernity) reveals is not the death of genre but its
proliferation. There are thrillers, in their various sub-genres including
gothic, spy, and murder mystery; there's *film noir*; there are buddy-
movies and women's movies and variations on both, like *Thelma and
Louise*. There are modern epics (and the epic-tragic love story of
Titanic) and even animated versions of classical epics. The customers
at the video store may not know which flick to pick, but they know the
sort of experience they want. Maybe they want to be scared out of their
pants, in which case they'll choose the one about the guy in a hockey
mask, or reassured by the victory of good over evil, in which case they'll
choose the one set long long ago in a galaxy far far away. *Friday the
Thirteenth* plays with its conventions and fulfils its viewers' expectations just as *Star Wars* does—and both movies are wonderfully self-
conscious about their manipulations of convention and expectation.
Our reception of films, whether they are the synergized product of a
media factory or the personal vision of an *auteur*, still depends on
'tradition: a sequence of influence and imitation and inherited codes
connecting works in the genre'.[1] The genres lumped under Drama in
the video store tend to play according to rules as rigid as any neo-
classicist assumed for tragedy. The same revelation awaits me at the

book store in the mall: from Self-help to Novel, from Spirituality to Crime, the whole place is a palace of codified notions of how our many modern genres work.

The dearth of modern works that call themselves tragedy is attributable to various complex causes. Perhaps our culture no longer believes in the kind of causation, moral or otherwise, which is required for an older tragic sense that a significant action has worked itself through to a necessary end. Death, like life, may seem random in a universe of quarks and quantum leaps; it is all too 'common' in the world of the holocaust and ethnic cleansing. Or perhaps we no longer believe in the outstanding individual whose fate, in other cultures than ours, produced the experience of pity and fear. Occasionally the old idea of the outstanding individual emerges in our response to real events, like the death of a president or a princess. But our social order is as likely to challenge as to underwrite the notion that some individuals are by nature more outstanding than others. Miller's *Death of a Salesman* is the tragedy of Willy Loman; it insists that attention must finally be paid to the low-men whose sad fates are written not in the stars or in themselves but in the inequities of the capitalist economic system. It is a touching effort to re-create an idea of tragedy for a world in which nobility has nothing to do with being born noble. But whatever the specific cultural causes, the modern dearth of works that even purport to be tragedies should not be surprising: comedy is always with us, in the depths of economic depression (the golden age of Hollywood comedy) as well as in palmy days, but tragedy (of the sort that can still engage audiences) seems to require special cultural circumstances for its production. It flourished in ancient Athens and again in the Renaissance. The real question is not, Why not now? but, Why then?

As the word tends to get used today, the idea of 'genre' suggests a minor work that hews to a limited set of conventions. A 'genre' novel (mystery, 'true romance', coming-of-age) may be the best in its kind, but the modern idea is that great works belong to no specific kind at all. As we've seen, such a notion would have been unintelligible to Shakespeare and his contemporaries, who saw the genres not as limiting forms but as opportunities for inventiveness.

A second answer to the question of the fate of genre: ancient genre theory has become modern genre theory; and since modern genre theory is an academic subject, it is, by definition, an area of considerable contention. In the twentieth century the idea that works can profitably be studied in terms of the conventions and traditions of genre has been both attacked and defended. The so-called New Critics of the post-Second World War period found little use for the idea of genre. They were committed to the individuality of the particular literary work as a formally coherent structure which held in tension the ambiguities and ironies it generated internally. To set a work in a tradition of similar works would diminish its uniqueness; to search for its 'meaning' in history, or in the work's own references to the historical world, would limit its potential play of ambiguity and irony. But for all the triumphs of sharp reading produced by the best of the New Critics, the effort to oust history (including the history of genres) is ultimately self-defeating. Historical contexts can multiply and enrich the kinds of ambiguities, ironies, and formal complexities the New Critics most prized. And, as this book tries to make clear, the idea of genre ought not to be a dictator of meanings or responses (if it's a comedy it's got to end happily, and if you don't laugh you've read it wrong) but a way to see how a work's originality is wrested from old materials, from the reworking of traditions, from the surprises and satisfactions that come from playing old games in new ways.

If genre theory had its enemies in the twentieth century it also had its friends. The strongest response to the anti-genre camp came in the monumental but always fluid, dazzlingly inclusive work of Northrop Frye. In *Anatomy of Criticism*[2] and the books—several of them about Shakespeare—which followed that summa, Frye connected the formal idea of genre to theories of myth and 'archetypes', finding, for instance, correspondences between the genres and the cycles of the seasons. Frye's enormous influence depended equally on the inclusive schematism of his system and its flexibility. Frye claimed a scientific objectivity for his anatomy of all literature, but on closer inspection his cycles and tables and charts of literary elements turn out to be as wonderfully idiosyncratic and un-reproducible as the best criticism should be. In recent years Frye has fallen out of favour, partly because we absorbed much of what he had to say, and partly because renewed interest in historical specificity makes his universalizing project seem insufficiently grounded in specific cultural forms. Recent historicist criticism of Shakespeare, including feminist and materialist criticism, tends to seek out the heterodox or the exceptional in culture; it can find the idea of genre too normalizing for its purposes.

But that same historicism must also lead us back to the Renaissance idea of dramatic genre. For Shakespeare and his contemporaries, the division of the plays into comedy, history, and tragedy was not a mere convenience but the reflection of deep habits of mind: the genres expressed fundamental ways of ordering the world and, by ordering it, of making it known. The great Globe theatre and the video store have that much in common.

I. THE GENRES IN THEORY

1. *The Thurber Carnival* (New York: Harper, 1945), 60–3.
2. This is the running-headline that appears in the Quarto edition (1600).
3. Jonson, *Discoveries*, ll. 2631–3, in *Ben Jonson*, ed. C. H. Herford, Percy Simpson, and Evelyn Simpson, viii. (Oxford: Clarendon Press, 1947), 643.
4. Johnson, *Rambler*, 125, quoted Alastair Fowler, *Kinds of Literature: An Introduction to the Theory of Genre and Modes* (Cambridge, Mass.: Harvard UP, 1982), 42.
5. Dryden, Preface to *Troilus and Cressida* (1679), in *Of Dramatic Poetry and Other Critical Essays*, ed. George Watson (London: Dent, 1962), 240.
6. Fowler, *Kinds*, 42.
7. *New York Times*, 29 May 1997, C16
8. Stephen Orgel, quoting Thomas Platter, in Orgel's 'The Comedian as the Letter C', in Michael Cordner, Peter Holland, John Kerrigan, eds., *English Comedy* (Cambridge: Cambridge UP, 1994), 36.
9. Whetstone, *Promos and Cassandra*, in Geoffrey Bullough, ed., *Narrative and Dramatic Sources of Shakespeare's Plays*, ii (London: Routledge and Kegan Paul, 1958), 443.
10. Bullough, *Narrative and Dramatic Sources*, viii (1975), 199.
11. *An Apology for Poetry*, in *Elizabethan Critical Essays*, ed. G. Gregory Smith (London: Oxford UP, 1904), i. 199.
12. Scholars' Facsimile edition (New York, 1938), introduction by Don Cameron Allen, pp. 2, 238.
13. Ibid. 281–2.
14. Horace, *Ars Poetica*, 92. For Jonson's title-page, see *Ben Jonson*, ed. Herford and Simpson, ix. 15–16.
15. Ibid. viii. 319.
16. *An Apology for Poetry*, written about 1583, published 1593, in *Elizabethan Critical Essays* ed. Smith, i. 199.
17. Ibid. i. 175.
18. *Discoveries*, ll. 129–38, in Herford and Simpson, viii. 567.
19. *Aristotle's Poetics: A Translation and Commentary for Students of Literature*, Leon Golden (Englewood Cliffs, NJ: Prentice-Hall, 1968), 15.
20. *Poetics*, trans. Golden, 10.
21. *Discoveries*, in Herford and Simpson, viii. 646–7.

22. Pope, 'Essay on Criticism', 1. 139–40.
23. The quotations are from Golden's translation of *Poetics*, in order: pp. 5, 26, 9.
24. Ibid. 11.
25. The first alternative is given in the translation by Gerald F. Else, *Aristotle: Poetics* (Ann Arbor: Univ. of Michigan Press, 1967), 25, the second by S. H. Butcher, *Aristotle's Theory of Poetry and Fine Art* (1894, 4th edn., 1907; repr. New York: Dover, 1951), 23.
26. Golden, 22; Else, 38; Butcher, 45.
27. Trans. by S. Georgia Nugent, 'Ancient Theories of Comedy: The Treatises of Evanthius and Donatus', in *Shakespearean Comedy*, ed. Maurice Charney (New York: New York Literary Forum, 1980), 259–80. (The short treatise attributed to Donatus may in fact be a composite of his work and that of another grammarian, Evanthius. It is analysed and translated as such by Nugent.) Quotations in this paragraph are from Nugent, 268–72.
28. In Bullough, *Sources*, ii. 443–4.

2. THE GENRES STAGED

1. *A Warning for Fair Women*, ed. Charles Dale Cannon (The Hague: Mouton, 1975), Induction, ll. 50–7.
2. *Cambyses*, sc. 10, ll. 215–16, 221–8, in *Drama of the English Renaissance* i: *The Tudor Period*, ed. Russell A. Fraser and Norman Rabkin (New York: Macmillan, 1976).
3. Sidney, *An Apology for Poetry*, in *Elizabethan Critical Essays*, ed. G. Gregory Smith, 2 vols. (London: Oxford UP, 1904), i. 199.
4. Ibid. 197.
5. *Gorboduc, or Ferrex and Porrex*, ed. Irby B. Cauthen, Jr. (Lincoln, Nebr. Univ. Nebraska Press, Regents Renaissance Drama Series, 1970), 3. 1. 165–8, 170.
6. Nashe, in Robert Greene, *Menaphon* and Thomas Lodge, *A Margarite of America*, ed. G. B. Harrison (Oxford: Basil Blackwell, 1927), 9.
7. Eliot, Introduction to Thomas Newton, ed. (1581), *Seneca His Tenne Tragedies, translated into English* (1927, repr. Bloomington, Ind.: Indiana UP, n.d.), p. xv.
8. Ibid., p. xxi.
9. *The White Devil*, ed. John Russell Brown (London: Revels Editions, 1960, 1966), 2–3.
10. *Cambyses*, in Fraser and Rabkin, *Drama*, i, sc. 2, ll. 25–6.
11. *The Complete Plays of Christopher Marlowe*, ed. Irving Ribner (New York: Odyssey Press, 1963).

12. Quoted in Paul H. Kocher, *Christopher Marlowe: A Study of his Thought, Learning, and Character* (New York: Russell and Russell, 1962), 35.

13. F. P. Wilson, *Elizabethan and Jacobean* (Oxford: Clarendon Press, 1945), 90, quoting R. Braithwait, *The English Gentleman* (1562), 109.

14. Fredson Bowers, *Elizabethan Revenge Tragedy* (1940; repr. Gloucester, Mass.: Peter Smith, 1959), 82.

15. *The Spanish Tragedy*, ed. Philip Edwards (London: Methuen, 1959), I. i. 90–1.

16. *The Poems of Sir Walter Ralegh*, ed. Agnes Latham (London: Routledge and Kegan Paul, 1951), 51–2.

17. *Ralph Roister Doister*, in William Tydeman, ed., *Four Tudor Comedies* (Harmondsworth: Penguin, 1984), Prologue 5.

18. *Gallathea*, in *The Plays of John Lyly*, ed. Carter A. Daniel (Lewisburg, Pa.: Bucknell UP, 1988), Act I, Scene I, pp. III–12.

19. Ibid. 201.

20. Ibid. 149.

21. William Empson, *Some Versions of Pastoral* (1935; new edn. New York: New Directions, 1974), 33–4.

3 . MR WILLIAM SHAKESPEARE'S COMEDIES

1. Donatus, trans Georgia Nugent, in 'Ancient Theories of Comedy: Evanthius and Donatus', in *Shakespearean Comedy*, ed. Maurice Charney (New York: New York Literary Forum, 1980), 271.

2. The most ingenious and extensive explorations of the connections between genre and myth are by the critic Northrop Frye in *Anatomy of Criticism* (Princeton: Princeton UP, 1957). For more about Frye in relation to Shakespeare studies, see the 'Epilogue' and the guide to Further Reading at the end of this book.

3. I quote this line (5. 1. 409) from the only authoritative early text, the First Folio. The Oxford edition emends 'nativity' to 'festivity'.

4. *Shakespeare's Festive Comedy* (Princeton: Princeton UP, 1959, repr. Cleveland, 1963).

5. Johnson, 'Preface' (1765), *The Plays of William Shakespeare*, in *Johnson on Shakespeare*, ed. William K. Wimsatt, Jr. (New York: Hill and Wang, 1960).

6. *Gammer Gurton's Needle*, *Four Tudor Comedies*, ed. William Tydeman (Harmondsworth: Penguin, 1984), 1. 2. 75–9 (I have modernized the spelling).

7. John Maddison Morton, *Box and Cox: A Romance of Real Life* (1847).

8. *The Importance of Being Earnest*, in *The Complete Works of Oscar Wilde*, intro. by Vyvyan Holland (London: Collins, 1966), 383.

4. HISTORY

1. Many recent critics call the second tetralogy 'The Henriad', borrowing the term coined by Alvin B. Kernan, 'The Henriad: Shakespeare's Major History Plays', *The Yale Review*, 55 (1969), expanded in Kernan, ed., *Modern Shakespeare Criticism* (New York: Harcourt, Brace and World, 1970), 245–75.

2. Plausible claims have been made for Shakespeare's authorship of another history play, *Edward III*. See the editions by Eric Sams (New Haven: Yale UP, 1966) and, for a more temperate review of the evidence for a Shakespearian hand in the play's composition, Giorgio Melchiori (Cambridge: Cambridge UP, 1998).

3. Irving Ribner, *The English History Play in the Age of Shakespeare* (Princeton: Princeton UP, 1957), 9.

4. Nashe, *Pierce Penilesse His Supplication to the Divell*, in *The Works of Thomas Nashe*, ed. R. B. McKerrow (London: A. H. Bullen, 1904), i. 212.

5. *Edward II*, 5. 1. 8–14, in *The Complete Plays of Christopher Marlowe*, ed. Irving Ribner (New York: Odyssey Press, 1963).

6. E. K. Chambers, *William Shakespeare: A Study of Fact and Problems* (Oxford: Clarendon Press, 1930), ii. 326–7.

7. Here as elsewhere I emend the text of the Oxford Shakespeare by using the name 'Falstaff' where the editors use the name 'Oldcastle'.

8. *The Famous Victories of Henry the Fifth*, sc. 1, ll. 93–4, in Geoffrey Bullough, *Narrative and Dramatic Sources of Shakespeare's Plays*, iv (London: Routledge and Kegan Paul, 1962), 302.

9. Holinshed, *The Third Volume of Chronicles* (1587), in Bullough, *Sources*, iv. 195.

10. E. M. W. Tillyard, *Shakespeare's History Plays* (London: Chatto and Windus, 1944; repr. 1980), 61.

11. This is the case argued by Annabel Patterson, *Reading Holinshed's Chronicles* (Chicago: Univ. of Chicago Press, 1994).

12. Norman Rabkin, *Shakespeare and the Problem of Meaning* (Chicago: Univ. of Chicago Press, 1981).

13. Bullough, *Sources*, iv. 278.

14. 'An Homily Against Disobedience and Wilfull Rebellion', in *King Richard II*, ed. Andrew Gurr (Cambridge: Cambridge UP, 1984), Appendix 3, 216.

5. TRAGEDY

1. A. C. Bradley, *Shakespearean Tragedy* (1904) (New York: Fawcett Books, 1965), 15.

2. Frye, 'The Argument of Comedy', *English Institute Essays 1948*, ed. D. A. Robertson (New York: Columbia UP, 1949), 65.

3. *The Complete Plays of Christopher Marlowe*, ed. Irving Ribner (New York: Odyssey Press, 1963).

4. Philip Finkelpearl, *John Marston of the Middle Temple* (Cambridge, Mass.: Harvard UP, 1969), 160.

5. Johnson, note to his 1765 edition of Shakespeare, in *Samuel Johnson on Shakespeare*, ed. W. K. Wimsatt, Jr. (New York: Hill and Wang, 1960), 97–8. Other quotations in this paragraph are from the same pages.

6. Frye, *Fools of Time* (Toronto: Univ. of Toronto Press, 1967), 31.

7. On the problem of scepticism in Shakespeare, see the philosopher Stanley Cavell, *Disowning Knowledge in Six Plays by Shakespeare* (Cambridge: Cambridge UP, 1987, repr. 1995).

8. *The Dialogues of Plato*, trans. B[enjamin] Jowett (Oxford: Clarendon Press, 1871; 4th edn. 1953), iv. 555.

EPILOGUE

1. Alastair Fowler, *Kinds of Literature: An Introduction to the Theory of Genre and Modes* (Cambridge, Mass.: Harvard UP, 1982), 42.

2. Princeton: Princeton UP, 1957.

| *Further Reading*

CHAPTER I

A good general introduction to theories of genre is Heather Dubrow, *Genre* (New York: Methuen, 1982). More copious and sophisticated is Alastair Fowler, *Kinds of Literature: An Introduction to the Theory of Genre and Modes* (Cambridge, Mass.: Harvard UP, and Oxford: Clarendon Press, 1982). On Renaissance genre in particular, see the authoritative work of Madeleine Doran, *Endeavors of Art: A Study of Form in Elizabethan Drama* (Madison: Univ. of Wisconsin Press, 1954), especially chapters 5–8. A sharply written brief survey of Renaissance theory in relation to Shakespeare is Stephen Orgel, 'Shakespeare and the Kinds of Drama', *Critical Inquiry* (1979), 107–23. Rosalie Colie's *The Resources of Kind: Genre-Theory in the Renaissance* (Berkeley: Univ. of California Press, 1973) stresses the varieties of mixed genres, but principally in non-dramatic writing.

Leonard Tennenhouse, *Power on Display: The Politics of Shakespeare's Genres* (New York: Methuen, 1986) discusses Renaissance genres as reflections of underlying ideological structures. Critics have productively linked ideas about genre to ideas about gender: see, for instance, the pioneering works by Linda Bamber, *Comic Women, Tragic Men: A Study of Gender and Genre in Shakespeare* (Stanford, Calif.: Stanford UP, 1982) and Coppélia Kahn, *Man's Estate: Masculine Identity in Shakespeare* (Berkeley: Univ. of California Press, 1981).

The influential, stimulating, and engagingly written work of Northrop Frye (see the Epilogue to this book for some comments) remains valuable even if the grand systems of *Anatomy of Criticism* have outlived their usefulness. Frye's books specifically on Shakespeare include *Fools of Time: Studies in Shakespearean Tragedy* (Toronto: Univ. of Toronto Press, 1967), *A Natural Perspective: The Development of Shakespearean Comedy and Romance* (New York: Columbia UP, 1965), and *The Myth of Deliverance* (Toronto: Univ. of Toronto Press, 1983) on the 'problem plays'.

CHAPTER 2

Martin Wiggins's *Shakespeare and the Drama of his Time* (Oxford Shakespeare Topics, 2000) surveys the vast subject of Shakespeare's relations to his predecessors and contemporaries. The connection between Shakespeare and Christopher Marlowe is the subject of Thomas Cartelli, *Marlowe, Shakespeare,*

and the Economy of Theatrical Exerience (Philadelphia: Univ. of Pennsylvania Press, 1991) and (with the third member of the triumvirate included) James Shapiro, *Rival Playwrights: Marlowe, Jonson, and Shakespeare* (New York: Columbia UP, 1991). On historical backgrounds for Shakespearian tragedy, see Wolfgang Clemen's study of the development of dramatic language, *English Tragedy Before Shakespeare*, trans. T. S. Dorsch (London: Methuen, 1961). Two sophisticated studies of Senecan influence are Gordon Braden, *Renaissance Tragedy and the Senecan Tradition* (New Haven: Yale UP, 1985) and Robert Miola, *Shakespeare and Classical Tragedy: The Influence of Seneca* (Oxford: Clarendon Press, 1992). English drama of the period immediately preceding Shakespeare is the subject of David Bevington's *From Mankind to Marlowe: Growth of Structure in the Popular Drama in Tudor England* (Cambridge, Mass.: Harvard UP, 1962). The influence of the poet Ovid is the subject of William Carroll's *The Metamorphoses of Shakespearean Comedy* (Princeton: Princeton UP, 1985) and of Jonathan Bate's *Shakespeare and Ovid* (Oxford: Clarendon Press, 1993).

CHAPTER 3

Susan Snyder's *The Comic Matrix of Shakespearean Tragedy* (Princeton: Princeton UP, 1979) gives a lucid account of Renaissance theories of comedy, and in later chapters readings of specific tragedies as variations on comic themes: it is an important contribution to our understanding of Shakespeare's way of both using and mixing the conventions of genre. Always useful is the survey of Shakespeare and his contemporaries in M. C. Bradbrook, *The Growth and Structure of Elizabethan Comedy* (London: Chatto and Windus, 1955, new edn. 1973). C. L. Barber's very influential *Shakespeare's Festive Comedy* (Princeton: Princeton UP, 1959) analyses the earlier comedies in light of the festivals of misrule practised in the English countryside during Shakespeare's lifetime. For Barber, comedy serves as a kind of safety-valve to let off revolutionary steam. The Russian critic M. M. Bakhtin supplies a theoretical vocabulary which some Shakespearian critics have used to emend Barber's analysis: in what Bakhtin calls 'carnivalesque' comedy, the 'upper-bodily stratum' (in the individual, the decorous pretensions of the rational mind; in society, the governing authority) is successfully mocked by the 'lower-bodily stratum': see *Rabelais and his World*, trans. Helen Iswolsky (Cambridge, Mass.: MIT Press, 1968).

    Several critics have discussed the history and implications of cross-dressing in Shakespearian comedy: see Lisa Jardine's *Still Harping on Daughters* (Brighton: Harvester, 1983), Stephen Orgel's witty essay 'Why Did the Elizabethan Stage Take Boys for Girls' (*South Atlantic Quarterly*, 88 (1988): 7–29), and Phyllis Rackin, 'Androgyny, Mimesis, and the Marriage of the Boy Heroine on the English Renaissance Stage', in Elaine Showalter, ed., *Speaking of Gender* (New York: Routledge, 1989), 113–33.

Alexander Leggatt, *Shakespeare's Comedy of Love* (London: Methuen, 1974) provides excellent readings of individual comedies. Also concerned with the variety of Shakespeare's experiments with comic form is John Russell Brown's *Shakespeare and his Comedies* (London: 1957). On the romances, see Howard Felperin, *Shakespearean Romance* (Princeton: Princeton UP, 1972) and valuable comments in the introduction to Stephen Orgel's editions of *The Winter's Tale* (Oxford: Oxford UP, 1996) and *The Tempest* (Oxford: Oxford UP, 1983). David Bergeron, *Shakespeare's Romances and the Royal Family* (Lawrence, Kan.: Univ. of Kansas Press, 1985) gives a challenging account of topical issues in monarchical history which may have contributed to the form of the romances. The so-called 'problem plays' have been discussed along with the romances by R. A. Foakes, *Shakespeare, The Dark Comedies to the Last Plays* (London: Routledge, 1971) and with the tragedies by Terence Hawkes, *Shakespeare and the Reason* (London: Routledge, 1964). The relation of pastoral conventions to comedy and romance are the subjects of David Young's *The Heart's Forest* (New Haven: Yale UP, 1972). A major study of Renaissance satire is Alvin B. Kernan's *The Cankered Muse* (New Haven: Yale UP, 1959).

CHAPTER 4

Classic studies of the history plays are E. M. W. Tillyard, *Shakespeare's History Plays* (London: Chatto and Windus, 1944) and Irving Ribner, *The English History Play in the Age of Shakespeare* (Princeton: Princeton UP, 1957), both of which associate Shakespeare's development of the genre with orthodox Tudor political ideas. (Robert Ornstein's *A Kingdom for a Stage* (Cambridge, Mass.: Harvard UP, 1972), by contrast, tried to dissociate the history plays from politics in order to view them as aesthetic objects.) John Wilders's *The Lost Garden: A View of Shakespeare's English and Roman History Plays* (London: Macmillan, 1978) provides a good introduction to its subject, as does Alvin B. Kernan, 'From Ritual to History: The English History Plays', in *The Revels History of Drama in English* (London: Methuen, 1975), iii. 262–99. Alexander Leggatt, *Shakespeare's Political Drama* (London: Routledge, 1989) has valuable readings of the individual plays.

A powerful challenge to Tillyard's construction of a 'providentialist' Shakespeare is mounted by Henry Ansgar Kelly, *Divine Providence in the England of Shakespeare's Histories* (Cambridge, Mass.: Harvard UP, 1970). More recent criticism has also tended to be sceptical of Tillyardian orthodoxy: see for instance Graham Holderness, Nick Potter, and John Turner, *Shakespeare:*

The Play of History (Basingstoke: Macmillan, 1988); and Phyllis Rackin, *Stages of History: Shakespeare's English Chronicles* (Ithaca, NY: Cornell UP, 1990), which discusses 'female subversion' of the genre's 'patriarchal' structures. Stephen Greenblatt's 'new historicism' develops a nuanced approach to the relation between authority and subversiveness: a good introduction is his chapter 'Invisible Bullets', on *Henry IV* and *Henry V*, in *Shakespearean Negotiations* (Berkeley: Univ. of California Press, 1988). Ivo Kamps, *Historiography and Ideology in Stuart Drama* (Cambridge: Cambridge UP, 1996) distinguishes several strands of English Renaissance history-writing and provides a sophisticated analysis from a modern theoretical perspective. The major recent study of Shakespeare's principal source for the history plays is Annabel Patterson, *Reading Holinshed's Chronicles* (Chicago: Univ. of Chicago Press, 1994). On *King John*, see the excellent introduction by A. R. Braunmuller to his edition of the play (Oxford: Oxford UP, 1989).

CHAPTER 5

Modern criticism of the tragedies begins with—or Victorian criticism culminates in—A. C. Bradley's *Shakespearian Tragedy* (many reprints since the original publication in 1904, e.g. New York: Fawcett Books, 1965), which finds a kind of secular redemptiveness in the plays' representations of suffering. At an opposite pole is the late twentieth-century materialist criticism of Jonathan Dollimore, *Radical Tragedy* (Brighton: Harvester, 1984), which finds in the plays of Shakespeare and his contemporaries an unmasking of the real social conditions which produce suffering.

J. V. Cunningham's brief but suggestive *Woe or Wonder: The Emotional Effect of Shakespearean Tragedy* (1951, repr. Denver: Swallow, 1964) considers the affective dimension of tragedy, while Robert N. Watson's longer book, *The Rest is Silence: Death as Annihilation in the English Renaissance* (Berkeley: Univ. of California Press, 1994) approaches the genre from a more philosophical direction. A useful study is David Young, *The Action to the Word: Structure and Style in Shakespearean Tragedy* (New Haven: Yale UP, 1990). A stimulating collection of feminist essays appears in Shirley Nelson and Madelon Sprengnether, eds., *Shakespearean Tragedy and Gender* (Bloomington, Ind.: Univ. of Indiana Press, 1996); also see Dympna Callaghan, *Woman and Gender in Renaissance Tragedy* (New York: Harvester Wheatsheaf, 1989), which considers *King Lear*, *Othello*, and two tragedies by John Webster. Lawrence Danson, *Tragic Alphabet: Shakespeare's Drama of Language* (New Haven: Yale UP, 1974) considers the tragic character's effort to achieve satisfactory expression. The idiosyncratic and sophisticated essays by the philosopher Stanley Cavell, in *Disowning Knowledge in Six Plays by Shakespeare* (New York: Cambridge UP, 1987) are highly rewarding for persevering readers. On the issue of tragedy in our own time (which I touch on in the Epilogue to this book) see Raymond Williams, *Modern Tragedy* (Stanford, Calif.: Stanford UP, 1966). Part of Williams's book is a challenging critique of 'modern' genre-theory through the first half of the twentieth century.

Index